NOF

The Quiet Struggle

Libraries and Information for Africa

Paul Sturges and Richard Neill

MANSELL

LONDON AND NEW YORK

This book is part of the Information Adviser series edited by J. Stephen Parker.

First published 1990 by **Mansell Publishing Limited**
A Cassell imprint
Artillery House, Artillery Row, London SW1P 1RT, England
125 East 23rd Street, Suite 300, New York 10010, USA

British Library Cataloguing in Publication Data
Sturges, R.P. (Rodney Paul), *1945–*
    The quiet struggle: libraries and information for Africa.
    1. Africa. Libraries. Information services. Libraries
    information services
    I. Title II. Neill, Richard, *1953–*
    020'.96

    ISBN 0–7201–2019–5

Library of Congress Cataloging-in-Publication Data
Sturges, R.P. (Rodney Paul)
    The quiet struggle: libraries and information for Africa / Paul
Sturges and Richard Neill.
       p. cm.—(Information adviser)
    Bibliography: p.
    Includes index.
    ISBN 0–7201–2019–5
    1. Libraries—Africa. 2. Information services—Africa.
    I. Neill, Richard, 1953– . II. Title. III. Series.
    Z857.A1S78   1989
    027.06—dc20   89–12267
                                          CIP

Printed and bound in Great Britain by
Biddles Ltd, Guildford and King's Lynn

Contents

Introduction

The story of contemporary Africa is a story of struggles. First there was the struggle for political freedom, often, as in the cases of Kenya, Guinea-Bissau and Zimbabwe, prolonged and bloody, while in the cases of South Africa, Namibia and Eritrea, still being fought. Then there is the struggle to create new political institutions and administrative mechanisms that has often resulted in waste, corruption, intrigue, coups, dictatorships and, in some extreme cases, the murderous excesses of personal rule by a Bokassa, a Macias, or an Amin. There is the struggle for economic emancipation, bedevilled as it is by a colonial legacy, and the often confused and self-interested interventions of foreign aid donors, as well as the activities of an African elite who are sometimes more concerned with personal enrichment than the sufferings of their people. There is also the struggle to forge a cultural identity, and to present a truly African countenance to the world.

Many of Africa's struggles have been chronicled by the world's media, which never seem to tire of painting a picture of a continent on the verge of total disintegration. There is, however, another struggle, a quiet struggle that rarely makes newspaper headlines, that has failed to attract the attention of the cameras of press and television. It has not featured prominently in the flow of books, articles, pamphlets, research papers and consultancy reports that discuss Africa in such seemingly exhaustive depth and detail and with such apparent authority and conviction. This struggle is led by Africa's writers, publishers, educationists, broadcasters, film makers, journalists and computer specialists, as well as its library and information workers, and it is the struggle for information, the struggle for knowledge.

1

It is this struggle, the struggle for information and knowledge, that this book seeks to address. Although the book is primarily concerned with this issue as it directly affects library and information development, the authors believe very strongly that libraries cannot meaningfully be discussed in isolation. They have to be considered within the context of a total information environment which encompasses issues ranging from literacy to satellite communications. Furthermore, this book embodies the conviction that much of the conventional thinking on library and information development in Africa needs to be turned on its head. Such an assertion can only be made on the basis of an extensive re-examination that goes back to the roots of information generation, transmission and use within the specific context of Africa.

This is obviously a major assignment and the authors do not claim exclusive credit for the content of this re-examination. Indeed the need for this radical reappraisal has long been voiced by a highly talented minority of commentators on the library and information scene in Africa. While it is no doubt true that in the past much of the literature on this subject has tended to be conventional and repetitive, this minority of writers and thinkers are now starting to make significant contributions towards developing a new body of theory for Africa's libraries. The authors offer this synthesis as a further contribution towards the search for relevance.

The book deals exclusively with sub-Saharan Africa. South Africa has been excluded except where the iniquitous system of apartheid impinges on the information sector in adjoining countries. For different reasons North Africa is similarly omitted. This is primarily because the traditions and culture there are so distinctively different as to require a fundamentally different treatment. It is also true that the content of the book is derived mainly from the Anglophone parts of the continent, rather than those areas where French, Spanish, and Portuguese are the metropolitan languages in use. This is unfortunate and an acknowledged deficiency. Whilst there should be sufficient reference here to the information worlds of non-Anglophone Africa to indicate some of the ways in which their problems and solutions vary, it is to writers with a firm base in these languages that the reader must look for detail on library and information work in those regions. Fortunately there is a real sense in which many generalizations hold good for more than one African country, despite the rich social and cultural diversity that exists. The authors have sought to identify examples of these widely applicable generalizations, and this is the basis of their claim to write about the library and information scene throughout Africa.

The book is written primarily for the attention of those directly concerned with information in Africa. The intention has been to present the arguments and proffer the solutions most likely to solve some of Africa's information problems. The book is intended to be of interest, not only to librarians, but also to writers, publishers, educators, communications workers and many others for whom information, whether they realize it or not, plays an important part in their everyday lives. Because of the intense and often committed interest in Africa to be found in many other parts of the world, it is also expected that some of the arguments presented here will be of interest outside the continent itself.

Acknowledgements

We wish to make grateful acknowledgement to Loughborough University for granting study leave to Paul Sturges during the first half of 1988 and to the African Studies Center at Boston University for awarding him visiting scholar status during that period, also to the University of Botswana for granting Richard Neill study leave during the second half of 1988 and Loughborough University for providing him with research facilities during his leave. Richard Neill is also very grateful to the German Foundation for International Development (DSE) for the many opportunities they have given him to increase his knowledge of African library and information work through research and travel.

We wish to acknowledge our debts of gratitude to many individuals. Professor Peter Havard Williams, whilst he was successively Head of Department of Library and Information Studies at Loughborough University and the Department of Library Studies at the University of Botswana, gave both of us encouragement and help on many occasions. Professor Jack Meadows, his successor as Head of the Department of Library and Information Studies, Loughborough University, also gave us both every assistance during the time we were writing this book. Colleagues in Gaborone and Loughborough frequently provided ideas and advice and gave practical help by covering our responsibilities during study leave.

Over the years during which our ideas were taking shape, so many students from all over Africa and from other parts of the world provided us with inspiration that it is impossible to thank them all by name. However, Richard Neill is particularly grateful to his seminar group at Loughborough University in the autumn of 1988 for discussion of drafts of chapters, and Paul Sturges much appreciated the comments of groups of faculty and students at the University of Pittsburgh and the University of California, Los Angeles, to whom he presented some ideas from work in progress.

Librarians at the University of Botswana, Loughborough University, Boston University and Southeastern Massachusetts University were all very generous with their assistance, but Paul Sturges is particularly grateful to Gretchen Walsh and Vicki Evalds of the African Studies section of Boston University Library and Shaleen Barnes of the Southeastern Massachusetts University Library for their especially valuable help. Goff Sargent and Andrea Kirkpatrick of the Department of Library and Information Studies at Loughborough University gave both of us invaluable guidance and support in our use of word processing systems.

Finally, Paul Sturges wishes to thank Gerard and Sheila Koot whose offer of a house and computer exchange made it possible for him to spend his study leave in the USA.

Chapter One

Africa's Information Environment

Introduction

In 1986, at around the time when the world's attention was drawn to the horrific starvation that was taking place in Ethiopia, the historian Michael Crowder was presenting a paper at the Standing Conference on Library Materials on Africa (SCOLMA) Annual General Meeting which focused on Africa's other famine.[1] The famine he was referring to was the book famine, and the picture he painted was in its own way as dramatic as the scenes of starvation that were portrayed on the world's television screens. If not reversed, the famine that Crowder so graphically described has been alleged to have implications as disastrous for Africa's long-term future as the catastrophic absence of food does for the short term.

This case was dramatically put by Kenneth Kaunda when he warned Zambians that they were, as a people, heading for intellectual bankruptcy because of the impoverished and distressed state of the nation's book trades. Calling the situation a national tragedy, Kaunda lamented the virtual absence of books from the nation's bookshops as well as the quality of those few that were available, describing them as the relics and leftovers of the book world rather than its treasures and riches.[2] A similar situation apparently exists in Tanzania, where reputedly the publishing industry and book trade have virtually collapsed so that Dar es Salaam can no longer boast a single well-stocked bookshop. In addition, because of foreign exchange restrictions imposed by the Bank of Tanzania, very few books have been imported by the book trade directly for the last ten years or so.

In terms of books, this is certainly the context in which Africa's development is taking place and the future of her people is being shaped. It is a context which can be tragically witnessed by a casual visit to almost any rural primary school class where it is not uncommon to see thirty or more children sharing three or four old and battered textbooks, with no additional reading material available. It is a context in which the illiterate population may be as much as, or even more than 60 percent, but as one may imagine no exact figures are readily available. It is a context where an entire continent can claim over 11 percent of the world's population, yet only 1 percent of its book production, 1 percent of its newspaper circulation and 1 percent of its paper consumption.[3]

Africa's famine of published information, however, is not only due to the poverty which make books unavailable but is also caused by the propensity of some African governments to suppress information. Often information could be readily available but is withheld, and the fate of those seeking to expose it can sometimes involve the very severest penalties. A fairly recent example involves the pall of secrecy that surrounded the subject of Acquired Immune Deficiency Syndrome (AIDS) in East Africa during the mid-1980s. AIDS first hit the headlines in Europe and North America three or four years previously and was almost without exception characterized, by implication at least, as a 'gay plague'. Then the finger of blame for its spread was pointed to Africa after a team of American researchers went to East and Central Africa and concluded not only that AIDS was endemic in the region but that its origins could be traced back to the local population. The fact that the tests that the researchers had used later proved to be unreliable was lost in the combination of media hysteria and public ignorance which convinced the world that Africa was the source of the AIDS menace.

The response of many African governments, particularly in East Africa, was, perhaps, at the time and in the circumstances, quite understandable. They refused to allow subsequent researchers to publish their results and the medical profession even had difficulty acknowledging that they were indeed treating patients who were suffering from AIDS. In Kenya, for example, there was an immediate restriction on the reporting of AIDS in the media and it was made fairly clear to Kenyan newspaper editors that there would be serious consequences if this embargo were to be broken. The results of these media restrictions were a burgeoning of rumour as to the cause and spread of AIDS, panic in the local population, the frightening off of visitors and tourists, and a belief amongst the Western press corps that its initial fears were being confirmed. A spiral of further sensational reporting in the world's press was the consequence.[4]

Another all too familiar example of Africa's information famine can be found in Cameroon, where the life of local journalists is made extremely unpleasant by the agents of the National Documentation Centre (CND), the secret political police, responsible for the effective enforcement of draconian censorship laws. As a result of their activities, reporting the news in Cameroon can be a rather dangerous occupation. The threat of arrest, detention and ill-treatment in the Nkolndengui political prison constantly hangs over those journalists who attempt to report anything contrary to the government's official line. Information as to what is actually going on in Cameroon has been so ruthlessly suppressed over the last twenty years or so, that the vast majority of its people now apparently rely on rumour, or the foreign media.[5]

Yet as counterbalance to these examples of information deprivation and distortion, there are positive features in the African scene. Viewed from a slightly different perspective Africa can be positively character-ized as information-rich. Travel in Africa, especially by bus, can be a disconcerting experience for the first time traveller or the unwary tourist. Trustworthy timetables don't exist and the bus will usually not leave until it is full, which may lead to a wait of an hour or more before the journey actually commences. Even then, several detours, delays and unscheduled stops along the way will usually occur, adding even more time to the journey. Despite the inconvenience, the delay in a sense serves a useful purpose as it enables Africa's own information system to function properly. In the constant talk and close inter-personal contact can be witnessed a highly complex information system at work. Its content covers a wide range of topics from the current market price for chickens to the prospect of Dan Quayle becoming the next President of the United States. Almost untouched by the technical complexities and expense of computer technology, or even by the diverse messages conveyed by books, Africa possesses a rich and adaptable mode of information transfer inherent in the social and psychological make-up of the people themselves.

Justifiable distress over Africa's book famine, or confidence in the resilience of traditional communication are, however, just two views that one can find frequently expressed by commentators. It is our contention that to see information in Africa as only represented by one or both of these two poles of poverty and wealth would be inadequate. Beginning with an examination of the oldest, yet still irrepressibly current method of information handling, in this chapter we will attempt to address the entire spectrum of information resources in Africa. The dramatic diversity of the ways in which information is handled in the continent is perhaps its chief attraction as a field of study. What is more, only from an appreciation of the various elements of the information environment, and the ways in which they co-exist, or fail to co-exist, can come any worthwhile analysis of the functioning and potential of library and information systems and services.

The oral medium

A totally oral society was until very recent times the norm in virtually every part of Africa. Despite the apparent influence of the printed word it still predominates, most notably amongst the rural population. Two types or levels of oral communication can be distinguished, the general and the specialized, each in its own way contributing to the strength of African culture and, what is important for our purposes, the information system and knowledge base which is an inseparable part of that culture. The general aspects of oral communication are those affecting people's everyday exchanges. They concern the ways in which information, ideas, and feelings are conveyed from one person to others. They involve the presence of subtle layers of added meaning arising from who is addressed, where, how, and by whom, as well as the use of gesture, tone of voice and particular modes of speech. The richness of Africa's oral culture in terms of its general characteristics can easily be witnessed wherever people meet, be it in the village, in the market place, or on some public mode of transport.

The more specialized aspects of oral culture can be defined by the ways in which society selects certain types of information for special treatment and public use, embodying them in formal patterns such as poetry, song and story. Accordingly the oral medium has acquired specialized practitioners such as story tellers, singers, praise poets and traditional healers who have had well defined roles and forums permitting the exposition of the communal knowledge and wisdom for which they are the major repository.

Given that this is the case, the questions 'What do the people know?' and 'How do they know it?' are of extreme importance and should really be answered. The honest answer is, however, that we probably don't know, at least with any degree of certainty, what is cumulated within Africa's oral culture. Obviously one can assume a fairly substantial body of knowledge about the environment and how to live in it. Over the years Africa's peoples have hoed the soils, grazed their animals on the land, hunted the game and collected the roots, leaves and fruits for medicinal purposes, until they have found when, where and how best to do all these things. They have discovered how to find scarce water and then how to conserve and use it to good effect. Local materials which might be suitable for building homes and other structures, making tools, clothing, furniture and other artefacts have been tried, tested and adopted. In this way a body of knowledge precisely adapted to the specific conditions of the particular locality has been assembled over the years which in turn has been enriched by the artistic, musical and spiritual heritage which constitutes a major part of the African milieu.

While, therefore, one can fairly easily identify and establish a base of indigenous knowledge, is this all and is it sufficient? The answer is probably 'No'. The oral tradition does not have an answer to everything, nor is it sufficiently pervious to knowledge from outside the immediate community. As an instance of this, Kingo Mchombu of the University of Botswana cites an example of a study undertaken amongst rural women in Central Tanzania. During the course of investigations related to the participation of women in rural development it was found that only 34 percent felt sure that malaria was caused by the bite of the mosquito. Many of these rural dwellers thought it was due to eating unripe maize or wild berries, and some even thought it was brought by the wind.[6] Malaria is not new to East Africa, nor is it uncommon in Central Tanzania. It is examples of ignorance like this that have led many to shun and even despise indigenous knowledge as shrouded in mysticism and superstition.

Certainly traditional knowledge and wisdom as embodied within an oral culture can be a problematical source, as has been discovered by the historians who have to date been the principal students of the medium. The work of Jan Vansina has long dominated the thinking on oral sources and between his earlier and later writings on the subject there are differences which reflect a changing appreciation of the difficulties of using the information contained in oral narrative.[7]

The oral medium cannot be treated as if it were directly analagous to written documents, for although documents may be open to a variety of interpretations, each interpretation is capable of justification on the grounds that it is based on equal access to the full written text of the original document. The oral narrative is not a complete and self-contained document in the same sense. As transcribed and often translated it represents only a particular version and lacks all the supporting apparatus of tone, emphasis and gesture which gives added meaning to the presentation. As told formally or in public, the narrative will have its own dynamic and content dictated by the nature of the occasion and the mood and response of the audience. In more private circumstances the same material would probably be presented in a more conversational manner permitting interjection, question and response to amplify and clarify the story. Without these features of presentation and performance the narrative is reduced to only part of itself and the comprehension of points which might confirm or invalidate a certain aspect thus becomes impossible.

Problematic as Africa's oral medium may be, it cannot be safely ignored, for the enduring traditions of the oral culture are still strongly discernible in present day Africa, clearly visible beneath the veneer of modernity. The challenge for all those who, even in the broadest of terms, are involved with information is to recognize that Africa possesses its own rich store of knowledge and its own highly developed modes of communication.

The oral tradition, however, is not only capable of providing answers from the past but can quickly respond to new ideas. Countless innovations from the bicycle to the transistor radio have been tested, adapted and finally absorbed into even the remotest parts of rural Africa. Even in remote rural areas the extent of 'modern' knowledge is invariably underestimated. Taking the example of political information, it has often been assumed that rural populations are politically ignorant even to the extent of not understanding what a vote actually is. The way in which difficult terrain, extremes of climate, poor roads and lack of vehicles limit travel and the contacts it brings, plus the absence of the modern information media that more developed countries can boast, tends to give this belief some plausibility. However, a number of surveys by no means bear this out, indeed they suggest something quite different.[8]

The ability of people in rural areas, literate or not, to name their political representatives and identify the content of issues of current political concern frequently outshines that shown by people in similar surveys conducted in the United States and Europe. Perhaps this could be explained away to some extent by the jaded appetite for political involvement which citizens in the West have developed as a consequence of the sheer volume of political information that confronts them both at election times and in the intervals between.

Perhaps also the comparative paucity of political information by Western standards in most African countries sensitizes people to what little is available and encourages them to retain and remember it. Whatever the reasons the basic findings remain and suggest the importance of oral communication in the political process.

The one bond that has linked together the colonial civil servant and the modern-day development planner is their lack of a proper appreciation of the strength of the information system and knowledge base which is an inseparable part of African culture. Values, beliefs, customs and traditional practices which the colonial administrators, traders, missionaries and settlers usually dismissed as being primitive and contemptible, were in fact rooted far back in time. Moreover, they had gradually been adapted to the needs, aspirations and imperatives of a society that had learned how to survive in an environment that could be severely hostile.

In more recent times there has been a tendency to view the people of Africa, particularly the majority who live in the rural areas, as the ignorant, passive and stubbornly uncooperative recipients of 'modern' information that has somehow been legitimized by the printed word. In particular, outside advisers and foreign aid donors, as well as administrators, politicians and those generally concerned with development issues, have often seemed to adopt the attitude that Africa's populace has little to offer in terms of ideas as to how their own future should be shaped. The actual position, though, is that the people probably have more idea than most, for within Africa's oral medium there exists a treasure-trove of knowledge which could contribute to the solution of many of the continent's persistent problems.

Radio and television

Oral transmission of information and the cultural and social norms associated with it is still undoubtedly of major significance and will no doubt continue to be so for the foreseeable future. It would, however, be foolish to place too big a premium on the oral tradition and to argue that it is the only medium of importance. In a survey of the political information received by Ghanaians it was found that about 30 percent credited people (politicians, chiefs, elders and travellers) as their usual source of information, while over 40 percent said that the radio represented their principal source of information.[9] It is perhaps with this in mind that it has sometimes been argued that radio and, to a lesser extent, television, have extended the scope of the oral tradition and are even enabling Africa to 'leapfrog' the literate stage to develop a more modern media-based society. Whilst this is undoubtedly facile and unconvincing, such is the significance of these media that they should be discussed next in this overview of Africa's information environment.

The importance of radio can be seen very clearly by the speed and extent of its spread. The proliferation of radio has largely been made possible by the invention and increasingly cheap availability of transistorized models. By interesting coincidence the advent of the transistor radio and the political independence of much of the African continent occurred at much the same time. Reliable figures for the number of receivers are not readily available, but the best estimates (excluding South Africa) suggest that from 1955 to 1985 there has been an increase from 360,000 to over 43 million individual radio receivers.

Governments have not been slow to appreciate that radio is the most significant mass medium available to them, nor for that matter have their opponents. It is perhaps no coincidence that, in the event of a coup, the nation's radio station is always a key point of conflict between the ruling regime and its opponents. In more peaceful times it has been a priority of many governments to extend transmission to as many people as possible and to use the radio not only to entertain but also as an instrument of policy. Often this has been in the form of outright propaganda and exhortation but it is not uncommon at the same time for radio to be used fairly extensively to communicate development-oriented information.

Positive views of this type of programming, dull as it often sounds to the outsider, are not too hard to find. For example, in Mali during the 1960s the Keta government turned to radio as a means of building a sense of nationhood, since the medium seemed quite appropriate for the pre-literate context in which it was going to deliver its message.[10] Political information supporting the policies of the ruling party did form an important element in news and current affairs programming, but what is interesting is how the folk tradition was also used for the same purpose. Baba Sissoko, one of Mali's most famous *griots* (or bards), had a weekly programme called 'Tales of Baba Sissoko'. His stories were reputedly much loved by the listeners and valued not only for their moral lessons but also for the glorious vision of the Malian past they inspired. This was done mainly through tales of the deeds of local heroes which were well calculated to encourage strong sensations of national pride. Families listened to the radio together and no doubt actively participated in the shared experience of this continuation and enhancement of the oral tradition. Examples like this of the ways in which radio has proved to be an effective medium for the dissemination of government policy, however unpopular the policy, could be multiplied from all over the continent.

Despite the generally optimistic and positive way in which radio is often described, scepticism about its potency as a medium for communicating information to support national development is not uncommon. The sceptical view begins by drawing attention to the misleading tendency to talk of radio as though it were universally available. Remote areas may receive no signal, or only a weak one, despite various efforts to improve transmission. Radio receivers, although undoubtedly cheaper today than ten or twenty years ago, are still an imported product for many countries which are already starved of the necessary foreign exchange. Mains power supply is still only confined to the relatively well off urban enclaves and even the cost of batteries can prove almost impossible for the rural dweller struggling to survive on a meagre subsistence wage. In addition to the problems of reception and cost, transmissions frequently fall below the standards required for the successful use of radio as an instructional medium. Under-funded services with too few trained staff are all too common and they are forced to take the easily available options for programming; a heavy diet of Western popular music, of the Michael Jackson variety, intermingled with the monotony of unedited political speeches and commentary.

When governments have planned to use media for development communication it has been to radio that they have usually turned. However, as Kwame Boafo has said of many such projects, they tend to be "short-lived, ad-hocish, limited in time and scope, and have not been sustained or built into a permanent national and comprehensive communication planning for development".[11] Boafo has also suggested that in fact the political elite pay lip service to the use of radio for development, whilst actually seeking to use it for their own preservation and aggrandizement.

Despite this the present status of radio is that it obviously plays a very effective role in providing entertainment. This makes it a familiar and acceptable part of people's lives. Because of this familiarity radio clearly does have a potential to contribute much more significantly to Africa's development. Nevertheless that potential has not yet been fully explored and radio remains only incidentally a medium for development information.

The growth of television, though much more limited in size and scope, has neverthless been quite rapid, with the number of receivers rising from zero in 1955 to an estimated 3 million thirty years later. Compared to radio, however, television is only narrowly available, being entirely the preserve of a comparatively rich urban elite. In addition, the expense and technical difficulty of creating sufficient programmes has led to an almost total dependence on the cheaper products of American television companies which dominate the screens of television viewers throughout Africa. The fictional adventures of characters in 'Dallas' and 'Dynasty' are as familiar to African viewers as they are to their counterparts in Europe and North America. Entertaining as these programmes no doubt are, they have nevertheless become yet another powerful instrument of cultural imperialism, with the message they convey being of extremely dubious value.

Films also confirm the hold of American entertainment corporations on African markets and the African consciousness. Films are expensive to produce, yet while India and other Asian countries have managed to develop massive film industries, creating entertainment in their own languages and cultural traditions, the story in Africa is distinctly bleak. With a few notable exceptions such as the works of directors like Ousmane Sembene and Med Hondo, who are almost all from the Francophone countries, Africa is virtually bereft of indigenous films. This in turn limits the scope of television to show films other than those bought from outside the continent.

Indigenous content on African television stations tends to be of variable quality, although at its best it can be highly informative and entertaining. For example, news output in many countries is governed by the natural principle that, to be broadcast, an item must be backed up with visuals. As a consequence, the majority of news departments, with limited news gathering facilities, become embarrassingly reliant on material available via satellite. This transmits the latest developments from London, Moscow and New York, rather than Lagos, Nairobi or Harare. The consequence of this is that African viewers receive live pictures of such events as the rioting of Liverpool supporters in the Heysel Stadium in Belgium during the 1985 European Cup Final, but are denied pictures of an All Africa Cup game between Nigeria and Morocco. Locally-produced entertainment material is limited by the technical capacity of the stations, with music programmes usually being the most straightforward. As a result these are often of a very high standard, and extremely enjoyable to watch. Stations do sometimes grapple with the complexities of broadcast drama. Some of the most interesting attempts can be witnessed on Nigerian television, which has captured (as far as this is possible) the exuberant improvisation of Yoruba traditional drama. It has also experimented with drama series, with 'Cock crow at dawn' a well-publicized example. Unfortunately such examples are the exception rather than the rule.

Whilst broadcast information may often assume an enhanced authority because of the medium which provides it, more commonly the lack of face-to-face communication and the facility for dialogue reduces its effect for the communication of development information. Surveys do indicate that people are still happier with personal contact as a means of acquiring practical information. Thus it would seem sensible to advocate traditional modes of communication, used in association with radio and other modern media, for the dissemination of development information. This can mean developing a broadcasting strategy centred around discussion groups and the informal gatherings that traditionally converge in African communities. The linking of mass media programmes with traditional media can mean harnessing the skills of story tellers, poets and musicians to include development-oriented information in their performances. Experiments have shown that the audience is far from unwilling to accept such types of information in a hybrid traditional form. The idea has a great deal of potential and as yet has only been used occasionally in Africa. What seems to be lacking is the will to integrate modern media with traditional modes of communication in long-term projects that could really exploit this potential.

The press in Africa

The history of the press in Africa can be traced back well into the early days of the missionary, colonial period, where, almost from the outset, successful newspapers were created by Africans to express the views of Africans. True, the circumstances in which this took place were not easy, for resistance to such efforts came from missionary, trader, settler and colonial civil servant alike. Nevertheless, against considerable odds an indigenous newspaper industry did develop. For example, the *Nigerian Times*, a nationalist newspaper founded in 1908, was the beginning of the extremely lively, highly politicized and largely privately-owned newspaper sector in Nigeria, which is still strongly in evidence today. Whilst most other countries had to wait a little longer for the emergence of similar enterprises, in all of them newspapers played an important part in the struggle for independence. Political parties and the trade unions often founded newspapers which could frequently boast contributions from future national leaders such as Julius Nyerere who was the *de facto* 'editor in chief' for the pre-independence *Mwaafrika* (which subsequently became the Swahili daily *Uhuru*), or Quett Masire, who started his career as a journalist for the now defunct *Naledi ya Botswana*.

The tradition of a press which was highly involved in politics and at least partly owned by political groups continued after independence. Since the press had played its part in winning political independence, it was perhaps natural that its role should subsequently be seen in the context of nation-building. African leaders recognized the potential of the press as a means of rallying the people towards a call for national unity and national development. The creation of government newspapers which could better put across this message was a natural consequence, and as a result although many countries still retain some semblance of a privately-owned press, in almost all cases it is the state-owned, government-controlled press that predominates.

The results have been disastrous, with the press now being almost exclusively used as a mouthpiece for the information which governments think that the people ought to hear.[12] The resulting tensions that exist between African governments and the press are too obvious and too well documented to be ignored. Journalists in Africa are often the first to be proscribed, interdicted, and detained at the first hint of unrest and instability. Self-censorship appears to be the key to survival in Africa and certainly evidence of a 'free' and critical press, as understood in the West, is not always easy to find.

On the other hand, most of Africa has had the good fortune to be spared from the worst type of stories that pass for news in the more sensational tabloids of the West. Despite the problems it creates for press freedom, the desire to have a press which performs an instructive function with national goals close to its heart is a valid one. Indeed, it is easier to justify than the artistic adornment of the pages of some of the more popular Western newspapers with pictures of semi-naked young women. The recent alliance of Robert Maxwell, whose British newspaper is not free of such excesses, and the Kenya African National Union (KANU), the single ruling political party in Kenya, with the intention of livening up the party newspaper, should result in an interesting product to say the least. One can hardly imagine how the typical story found in the *Daily Mirror* will appeal to the local KANU stalwarts in Kenya when they open their newspaper expecting to read the latest party news.

Despite this isolated example of the importation of Western press values, it is more common to argue that the African news environment is, and should be, different from that which operates in Europe and North America. A philosophy of 'development journalism' has been evolved to guide the efforts of those involved with the news. This philosophy, which is based on the idea that the press is too important to be allowed to follow the allegedly free, but frequently frivolous, course of newspaper publishing in the West, has attracted much criticism. Hostility towards the news policies of Africa has mainly centred around Unesco's 'New World Information and Communication Order', which is a call for not only a free but also a balanced flow of information between countries. There has been a strong feeling, in the West, that this has merely represented a ploy to further endorse government control of the press, reinforcing press censorship. The spectre has been raised of Western journalists being denied their accustomed freedom to move around and report what they want in the way they choose.

Whilst there is no doubt that many African governments would prefer to kill a story that reports them unfavourably, nevertheless the extent to which the Western media fail to come to terms with the realities of Africa is notorious and was a major reason why a new direction was felt to be necessary. The issue of how Africa is reported by the rest of the world is important. Reporters and cameramen fly in to cover an issue, usually a disaster like a famine, drought or flood, or one of Africa's periodic coups, provide dramatic stories for a few days or perhaps weeks, and then move on to the next global 'trouble spot'. Stories for which dramatic pictures are not available or which fail to confirm the prejudices of the newsmen's intended audience, are conveniently ignored. The way in which Ethiopia ceased to be headline news in the Western media almost overnight, despite the continuation of the drought and the resultant catastrophe that it caused, is perhaps sufficient to illustrate the point. It is as if news does not exist where it cannot be backed up by dramatic film footage or by lurid accounts of atrocities which portray Africa in an extremely negative way.

Some African governments have sought a quick remedy to these imbalances by locking up and expelling Western journalists. Fortunately, saner heads have sought a solution through the creation and development of better sources of news on Africa. The Pan African

News Agency (PANA), founded in 1983, is one of the means intended to supply the world with a consistent and reliable flow of information on Africa. It seeks to use modern satellite communication to provide editors with material that is less oriented towards dramatic events and more concerned with chronicling the development struggle. Unfortunately, positive initiatives such as this face not only the indifference and cynicism of the media they seek to penetrate, but also considerable technical constraints. Although satellite systems such as INTELSAT enable agencies like PANA to reach the news desks of the world, the tendency is increasingly for Western editors to ignore agency material which cannot be edited on-line and incorporated directly into their electronically produced newspapers. The low capacity telex channels used for material from Africa produce only hard copy, which unfortunately does not meet this requirement. The stories coming out of Africa are thus condemned for the most part to form a part of the vast majority of material which is received by newspapers but never used for publication.

Whilst the problem of how to improve the reporting of Africa outside the continent is proving to be extremely intractable, the coverage of Africa by itself within the continent is far from satisfactory. Surveys of the content of African newspapers have tended to show that their reporting of news from other African countries is slow and limited in scope. There is a sharp divide between Anglophone and Francophone Africa as far as the passage of news is concerned and stories from countries in the immediate region outnumber those from further afield. An analysis of the content of some Nigerian newspapers showed that between a quarter and a third of their stories consisted of foreign news and only about half of this was from other parts of Africa.[13] Since Nigerian newspapers and the News Agency for Nigeria, largely for financial reasons, had no reporters based in other African countries, these stories were obviously derived from other news agencies. This meant that the vast majority were obtained from the very Western agencies that Africa accuses of misreporting the continent.

Despite problems of government ownership, control, and censorship, the press, in particular the private press, is flourishing in a number of African countries such as Nigeria, Kenya and Botswana and is managing, at least in part, to tell the news. There are problems, however, even when this is possible. The private press in particular suffers from a lack of finance for equipment, and a dearth of newsprint. If, as is usually the case, newsprint is imported by the government, supplies can obviously be restricted in such a way that newspapers are forced to conform or close down. This is clearly an indirect form of censorship. The price of newsprint, when it can be obtained, is so high that it results in the sad paradox of newspapers being unable to produce sufficient copies to satisfy demand, because the revenue from the increased sales would not cover the cost of additional newsprint. Even when newspapers have managed to overcome these considerable hurdles, and the paper has been produced, circulation is mostly restricted to the cities and towns. In the rural areas distribution is usually unreliable and often only occurs when a traveller or migrant worker returns to the home village. Nevertheless, despite low levels of literacy, particularly in the rural areas, the press can still be a highly significant medium for development information in Africa. The fairly common practice of an individual reading the news to a group who may not themselves be able to read, multiplies the effective use of each copy. The listeners are quite capable of absorbing the content and passing it on even further through subsequent conversation.

In addition, examples can be found of worthwhile initiatives to make newspapers more effective. For instance, there are attempts to use new technologies to assist journalists in getting their message across to the rural areas. A recent initiative is in Zimbabwe, where the latest techniques in desktop publishing are being used to produce a twice-monthly, eight-page tabloid, on cheap newsprint. The paper, entitled *Chaminuka News* and selling for ten cents, has been produced specifically for the rural inhabitants of Mashonaland East. It includes text in English and Shona, and stories in the first issue included a report on the oil-producing Macadamia tree, the opening of a new civic centre, guidelines on starting a co-operative, and instructions on how to use chemicals.[14]

Although examples like the above may not be commonplace, and while it must be admitted that often the press in Africa is a mouthpiece for government propaganda, nevertheless many journalists and editors are attempting to satisfy the public demand for information in a way that supports, rather than hinders, national development. It is to be hoped that the effort and persistence of the press will encourage African governments to accept, rather than fear, the publication of the truth. This in turn should lead to a lessening of the uncritical reporting which presently characterizes much of the African media's reporting of Africa, and to a more balanced opinion being provided by the media of the West.

Books and publishing

If the outlook for newspapers in Africa appears to be slightly encouraging, the present position of the book can only be described as depressing. The poverty of book resources in Africa has been well chronicled in terms both of lack of demand and inability to meet such demand as there is. Thus the weakness of the booktrades has been variously attributed to massive illiteracy, the lack of a reading culture (even amongst the present generation of educated Africans), lack of book production skills and equipment, poor library and distribution networks, trade barriers and closed markets and the economic dependence of the book trade, as well as to the political, cultural and linguistic divisions of the African continent. It is perhaps not too surprising, therefore, that when confronted with this formidable list of obstacles, the book has failed to play a significant role in the social and cultural development of the continent and its people.

In an attempt to quantify Africa's acute shortage of books, Robert Escarpit came to the conclusion that the figures that are available are so low that any form of comparison or quantitative analysis is virtually impossible.[15] This judgement was subsequently confirmed by Unesco when during the course of an international survey of book production it was noted that "of the 55 countries and territories included under Africa, a few only produce books. And of those, a smaller number report their statistics to Unesco. Many of the countries do not have a depository system and would be at pains to produce statistics on book production, even if there was any".[16] This is, then, an unrelievedly gloomy picture of a continent apparently uninterested in publishing and not having books in sufficient numbers and presumably of sufficient quality for the needs which are apparent.

If we examine the origins of African publishing we find that it was originally a means for producing and distributing educational and missionary texts written by non-African authors. The publishing of books by African writers can only really be traced back to the 1950s when a number of aspiring young authors with manuscripts in the metropolitan languages began to be published with some frequency. In the Francophone countries this was welcomed and indeed encouraged by an organization specifically devoted to that purpose, the Institut Français de l'Afrique Noir. This effort was complemented by the setting up of a publishing house in Paris, Presence Africaine, which was largely responsible for bringing to public attention the writings of the poet Leopold Senghor and the novelists Camera Laye and Mongo Beti.

The system in the Anglophone countries was not nearly so supportive, with the local branches of British publishers showing little interest in publishing non-textbook material written by Africans. Undeterred, a number of these writers bypassed this obstacle and were able to attract the attention of a few publishers in London who fortunately recognized their talents. The initial breakthrough was made by West African writers, notably with Amos Tutuola's *The Palmwine Drinkard* in 1952, and Chinua Achebe's *Things Fall Apart* in 1953. In the 1960s it was the turn of East Africa, with the works of James Ngugi, David Rubadiri and Okot p'Bitek appearing in print. In bringing the work of these writers to a world readership, publishers such as Faber, Oxford University Press, André Deutsch and Heinemann undoubtedly performed an important service in nurturing and developing Africa's creative writers. At the same time though, as a consequence of their efforts, they effectively detached some of the best talent from its roots, which in turn probably did a disservice to the prospects for a strong, commercially sound African publishing industry.

The patterns of publishing now to be found around the continent are still broadly similar, with the international publishing houses maintaining the upper hand. They retain considerable ability to determine what and who ought to be published, and ultimately what should be read about Africa. At the advent of independence local branches of publishers such as Longmans, Nelson, Evans and Heinemann registered as companies in the countries in which they were operating while at the same time increasing the level of local participation in their activities. For instance, by 1963 the Nigerian branch of Oxford University Press was able to handle the whole publication process of locally-written books and publish its own titles under its own imprint. The only element which could not be said to have been localized was the resultant profit from these titles, which continued to be exported back to the parent company.

Some international companies set up new local operations in which they maintained a minority holding, with the most notable examples being African Universities Press based in Lagos, and the East African Publishing House with its headquarters in Nairobi. Both were initiated by André Deutsch, with the latter managing fairly quickly to dispense with any outside involvement to pursue a highly creative policy as an indigenous publishing house. State publishing houses developed along similar lines, with Macmillan in particular playing an important role in Ghana, Uganda, Tanzania and Zambia. Similar arrangements developed in the Francophone countries, where, for example, Ivory Coast and Senegal shared a controlling interest in Nouvelles Editions Africaines, with a group of French publishers making up the minority stockholding.

State publishing houses were conceived of originally as being similar in their role to the government-controlled newspaper press, with the overt aim of fostering unity and national development. The results have been far from convincing and in some cases disastrous. Many were established as a result of controversial agreements with international publishers, with Macmillan seeming to be the main target for criticism. The usual sort of deal apparently provided the international publisher with a closed market in the countries with whose state publishing houses they were co-operating.[17] Such agreements now seem to be a thing of the past, though their legacy lingers on. The tenacity of international publishers to hold on to what must be a comparatively unimportant market on the world scale has helped to ensure that Africa remains a captive market for their products, while at the same time stifling attempts at local publishing initiatives.

The strength of the international publishers is such that after more than two decades of independence the 'best' African writers almost all choose to publish their work outside the continent. The strong attraction, to writers, of signing agreements with major international publishers is obvious. It not only gives them the chance to communicate with a vast worldwide readership, but also to travel on highly lucrative lecture tours and be offered writers' fellowships at prestigious universities, as well as ensuring higher and more reliable financial rewards, usually in the form of precious foreign currency. Books by the most successful writers have no doubt gained from their publication by international publishers, some of whom specifically promote African writers, as Heinemann have done with their African Writers Series. But the main purpose of such efforts is to identify and promote a limited number of 'outstanding' titles for the convenience of book buyers in the developed countries. The African market tends not to be a major priority in determining what shall or shall not be published and the limited outlet provided by international publishers for Africa's creative talent is no substitute for the broad development of African writing that is necessary to alleviate the endemic book hunger.

It is not, therefore, to the international publishers that we must look for the creation of a book market in which new writers can learn their trade and seek to expand the definition of what constitutes an African writer. This makes it important to examine other publishing patterns that are emerging throughout the continent and which, against the odds, are beginning to create a truly indigenous African book industry. It is to the informal sector that one must turn if the real heart of African publishing is to be discerned.

This sector is best known in Nigeria, where the once famous 'Onitsha market literature' gained, quite a few years ago, some attention from the book world. This publishing phenomenon consisted of simply printed and bound, locally-written books. They were sold outside the conventional book trade, from pavement stalls and kiosks, in shopping malls and traditional markets, in buses and along the streets, in Onitsha as well as other major towns and cities such as Ibadan, Lagos, Aba, Port Harcourt and Enugu. While the Onitsha market literature did at one time arouse a certain level of attention, it has received little detailed study.[18] At its best it represents a lively and spontaneous reaction to an obvious demand from African readers. The stories have enjoyable titles like *True love: Fineboy Joe and Beautiful Cathe* (described as 'Our modern ladies character towards boys: the most exciting novel with love letters, drama, telegram and campaigns of Miss Beauty to the teacher asking him to marry her'); *Mabel: The sweet honey that poured away* ('Her skin would make your blood flow in the wrong direction. She was so sweet and sexy, knew how to romance. She married at sixteen. But she wanted more fun. Yet it ended at seventeen. And what an end? So thrilling!'); *Make yourself extremely romantic* (A very literary, mystico-erotic drama published by the Wamoyega Institute of Perfection).

Writers in the informal sector often sell the copyright of their books to the publisher for a single payment only to find that the publisher proceeds to reprint the book, possibly under a new title, without acknowledging the author and almost certainly with no royalties being paid. To the publisher the stories are merely a product to be sold for a quick profit and the stories' refreshing lack of literary pretension obviously helps in achieving this objective. Booker Prize material they usually are not. A good read they certainly are.

Market literature is not the only spontaneous publishing initiative from Nigeria, 'photoplay' magazines being another. These are serialized versions of the prolific Yoruba popular drama, using still photographs of the characters with captions telling the story. The magazines do have a small amount of other content including pages of fiction, humorous commentary and penpal pages. These pages have the picture as well as a brief biography and address of the aspiring penpal. A study of them in a large number of these magazines would give a fascinating sample of their readership, but at a glance, students and semi-skilled workers, mainly lorry drivers, seem to predominate.

Neither market literature nor photoplay magazines make any unrealistic claims to artistic or literary merit, and they are not the kinds of enterprise to attract official or philanthropic subsidy or support. They are quite simply a response to a demand from ordinary people for information, advice and entertainment. The response is furnished by writers, printers, publishers, and booksellers, who quite often embody all the other three functions in the one person and whose own interests and socio-economic background are probably little different from those of the readers.

The evidence from such publishing initiatives in Nigeria shows that the reading society, which so many academics, librarians, educators, authors and publishers have bemoaned as not existing in Africa is, in fact, starting to emerge, if only they would recognize it. Unfortunately, it is being born under difficult circumstances and only a few scraps of evidence indicate that it has spread to other parts of the continent. The creation of an indigenous African publishing industry will for some time be greatly hindered, not only by the duopoly of state and international publishers whose role has frequently been described and agonized over,[19] but also by lack of finance. African entrepreneur publishing is heavily undercapitalized, has low profit margins and fails with great frequency. In these circumstances, bank credit is hard to obtain. In addition to the obvious financial difficulties, aspiring publishers find themselves involved in a multiplicity of tasks such as composition, presswork and binding, diverting their attention away from the actual business of publishing. Machinery, spare parts and materials such as paper, ink and offset plates are all in short supply and skilled workers are at a premium.

All these difficulties have produced an unstable and bibliographically problematic local publishing industry, with the less established sector being graphically described by J.U. Obasi in the following way,

> In general the printers are slow or even reluctant to give any information about their existence or origin. Some of them go into liquidation after a very short history of operation. The young entrepreneurs who own them appear to be nomadic moving from one shop or city to another within a few years. This is often due to financial reasons, to meet increased rates and electricity bills. Often they do not leave any contacting addresses and in

circumstances where these are known, the omission of the post office box numbers makes them impossible to locate.[20]

A librarian's point of view, but one can imagine the difficulties these fluctuating circumstances must cause for the writer, publisher, book buyer, materials supplier and, no doubt, for a list of creditors too.

Yet another intractable problem of book production and publishing in Africa is that of language, and this seems to be no nearer a solution with the passing of the years. Put quite simply, a continent with an estimated 1,000 languages or more is never going to be an easy publishing environment. Major languages do manage to achieve comparatively reasonable levels of publication. This however is only achieved in an international language such as Kiswahili (which has about 20 percent of all the new titles published in African languages), or the language of the major population group in Nigeria, Yoruba (with about 12 percent of new African language titles). The majority of the continent's languages have at the best a tiny published literature. Some have none at all, and indeed may not even have a written form or an established orthography. The missionary presses which were usually the first to publish in African languages often devised a clumsy orthography which led to many disputes not only amongst Africans, but also amongst the various missions. The legacy of this still lingers today, hindering the progress of writing and publishing.

The prestige of the old colonial languages, particularly English and French, has encouraged many writers to continue to use them. About 80 percent of new titles from Africa are in these languages, despite the fact that less than 5 percent of the continent's population is regarded as being really fluent in either of them. English is the more successful of the two languages, with approximately twice the number of publishers producing double the volume of new titles. This is perhaps not surprising as it serves the more populous areas and enjoys a worldwide currency. The majority of popular imaginative literature is produced in English and the number of titles produced in African languages is discouragingly small.

This problem of a dearth of material in the people's own language has worried most commentators on African publishing. Encouraging signs, such as Amos Tutola's decision to rewrite his *The Palmwine Drinkard*, originally in English, in his mother tongue, Yoruba, are few and far between. It has been suggested that the use of a foreign language makes it difficult for individuals to learn to read and to develop a reading habit. Yet when someone aspires to be an author they invariably have a tendency to want to write in a foreign language. Many solutions to the problem have been suggested and some have been tested in practice. For example, in the 1940s the East African Literature Bureau and the Publications Bureau of Northern Rhodesia and Nyasaland both set out to foster the publication of vernacular literature, textbooks and periodicals. The latter's intention was not to undertake the publishing itself, but to place manuscripts with suitable publishers and then assist with the distribution of the publications through "libraries, bookstalls, and colporteurs".[21] It did have some modest success over the years and successor organizations in Zambia and Malawi have carried on its work. But, like numerous other similar schemes, it never succeeded in promoting mass publication in Africa's many languages.

Yet another problem is the production of children's literature, which according to *African Books in Print* rarely exceeds more than a few hundred titles a year. This quantity of suitable children's material is nowhere near enough to satisfy the demand placed on it by Africa's comparatively youthful and rapidly growing population. By 'suitable' we mean material which is written with the African child in mind. This does not mean the exclusion of children's literature from other parts of the world, nor an embargo on non-African authors producing material appropriate for use in an African context. Rather it means that ideally the bulk of the material available for children should be written by African writers and at least some of it should bear a close relation to the conditions that the African child is likely to experience. Unfortunately, writing for children has not had a particularly high prestige amongst African authors, with only a few of the famous like Chinua Achebe, who (with John Iroaganchi) wrote *How the Leopard Got His Claws*, and Ngugi wa Thiong'o, whose *Njanba na Mbaathi i Mathagu* is written in Gikuyu, producing books suitable for children.

A few books of reasonable quality for young adults started to appear in the 1960s trying to emulate the success of Cyprian Ekwensi's *The Drummer Boy*. Such books have tended to take a rather obviously didactic line and, as has been pointed out in the case of Nigeria, "These novels reflect what Nigerian society wants Nigerian youths to be or what it does not want them to be".[22] This is a reassuringly familiar complaint from the youth of every generation and from every continent. The important thing is that there are attempts to develop a much needed market in books for young adults. A major proportion of this market has been taken up by international publishers, such as

Macmillan with their inexpensive 'Pacesetters' series of lively and appropriate stories written by African authors.

Unfortunately, there has not been a great number of African publishers with a strong interest in children's books. A few indigenous publishers such as Nouvelles Editions Africaines of Dakar, East African Publishing House of Nairobi and the Mazenod Centre in Lesotho are producing some good material, but the majority seem to have retreated from the inherent difficulties of producing children's literature and have abandoned the market to the international publishers. The problem is so grave that the Nigerian writer Florence Nwapa had to set up her own Tana Press to specialize in children's books. Initiatives like this, however, are few and far between and are unlikely to provide a proper solution to the lack of suitable reading material for children and young adults.

Money is once again the major problem, for publishing children's books is an expensive business, made difficult by the fact that the cover price should not be so exorbitant as to inhibit children or their parents from purchasing the book. Publishing at a low enough price can be achieved either by producing a long print run with the intention of selling large numbers of copies, or by saving money on the actual production of the book. The first option is extremely risky and it is to the second that most of the local publishers will be tempted to turn, resulting in an unattractive and easily damaged product. Children's book publishing in Africa needs to be well capitalized if local publishers are to compete with the richly endowed international publishers who presently dominate the market. The Noma Award for Publishing in Africa has been won by several books for children since it was first offered in 1973, but again, this can never be enough. The market for children's books is potentially enormous in Africa, the creative talent to write and illustrate the books is not lacking, nor is the expertise and even the capital to produce and publish them. What is lacking at the moment is the incentive and the will, and until a more assertive approach is adopted by African publishers, African children, who represent the continent's future, will continue to be denied the opportunity to read.

Information technology

The importation of information technology to Africa's urban landscape is clearly evident to the newly arrived tourist, business traveller,

expert, or foreign aid consultant. From their first arrival at the
international airport through to their stay at the nearest five star hotel,
as well as through visits to banks, offices and commercial enterprises,
visitors cannot help but become aware of the fact that computers have
made their entrée into Africa.

As to the question 'How many computers does Africa possess?' the
simple answer is quite probably that nobody really knows. What is
certain is that a place where one is unlikely to find much evidence of
the revolution in information technology is in Africa's libraries. Information technology has as yet left the African library profession largely
undisturbed. More important, moving outside the comparative
modernity of Africa's urban sprawl and into the rural areas, the
traveller finds a much older version of the paperless society. This
differs from Wilfred Lancaster's[23] vision of a paperless society, in that
not only is it paperless but also computerless. To the largely illiterate
population, anything they learn of information technology must seem
a meaningless aberration of 'modernity' that is of little help to them
in facing the grim realities of everyday life.

While it would be absurd to deny the potential of computers to
enhance and improve economic and social conditions in developing
countries, there are a number of areas of anxiety about these types of
technology in the African context. First there are the obvious ones
concerning the acquisition and use of what is a very complex technology. The sales forces of computer companies are renowned for their
willingness to sell unsuitable equipment to underprepared buyers. In
particular, the big American information corporations have placed a
great reliance on maintaining growth through the export of information goods and services. Similarly, the export-minded Japanese have
also aggressively pursued world markets in order to ensure that their
information technology products maintain their position as market
leaders.

It is in such a climate of pressure salesmanship that many African
governments have been encouraged to commit themselves to making
an investment in information technology as a means of providing an
electronic solution for their countries' myriad problems. The consequences are not always particularly acceptable ones. Whilst it can be
argued that Africa is merely fulfilling a natural desire to keep pace
with the rest of the world, the reality is that the import of the new
technologies merely constitutes, at present, a strong reinforcement of
Africa's dependence on the West.

At face value, the importing of information technology can be beneficial, enabling important functions to be performed in more effective ways. These include inventory control, accounting, payroll, improving telephone systems, handling of statistical data in government departments, or the management of development projects. However, since there is no significant computer or communications hardware manufacturing industry in independent sub-Saharan Africa, nor the necessary capacity to produce software, the result is that the machines not only have to be purchased outside the continent, but have also to be maintained, repaired, replaced and operated by agencies whose main base of operation is outside Africa.

The only 'fortunate' exceptions are the states in the vicinity of South Africa, a country which, in association with the West, has managed to develop a highly modern computer industry. The extensive use of computers by South Africa for the handling of data which permits the detailed administration and policing of its apartheid system is well known. That South Africa also appreciates the significance of computers that are in the hands of its opponents is evidenced by the military raid on Gaborone, Botswana, in June 1985. In addition to the killing and wounding of those they identified as being engaged in 'terrorist' activities, the intruders pointedly destroyed personal computers belonging to South African refugees. It is South Africa which controls the supplies of most of the new equipment, components, software, maintenance and technical backup to many of the frontline states, which hardly augurs well for any attempts at national or regional self-sufficiency in information technology.

In some ways, however, this merely points up the dependent relationship in which all African states find themselves over information technology. As long ago as 1979, at an Intergovernmental Bureau for Informatics (IBI) conference held at Abidjan, a number of African states were challenging America's right to the majority of the world's data bases which were held under the effective control of the large American corporations, Lockheed and Systems Development Corporation. This challenge was made despite their fear that as Africa's use of these data bases grew, any attempt to wrestle free from this dependent relationship could provoke a reaction resulting in restricted or curtailed access. In addition, those African countries present claimed the right to the information held in those data bases that was of African origin. Not surprisingly their request met with little sympathy.[24]

A second argument for caution in applying technology is marshalled by Anthony Olden.[25] He suggests that while the technical problems can be overcome and information technology can be made to work in developing countries, its application is of limited benefit to the populace as a whole. The concentration of resources which is necessary to apply information technology is likely, in the first place, to be paid for at the expense of services for the masses. The information which can be obtained by this means is mainly in the form of citations of material, the great bulk of which is not obtainable from within African countries. It can certainly be obtained via document delivery systems based in overseas countries (the British Library's Document Supply Centre, for instance) but again at considerable cost. Information obtained through such channels, it is suggested, is chiefly of benefit to quite a narrow, and already highly privileged, stratum of society. The filtering down of benefits from this information to the masses is likely to be limited in comparison with the gains that could be made from concentration of resources on broadly based services. This line of argument has at its core both a mistrust of those who already have the easiest access to educational and information resources and a certain scepticism about the value of the type of material which is available via data bases and document delivery systems. Pessimistic though it is, it reflects a valid fear about the trends that will emerge as information technology applications become more common in the continent.

The convergence of computer and telecommunications technology which permits transborder dataflow shares this potential to threaten rather than benefit Africa. The swift and accurate movement of financial information, invoices and freight documentation, personnel records, travel bookings, vital economic and geodetic data, as well as huge sums of money, over great distances, has obvious advantages as well as potential drawbacks. The major disadvantage is that many such operations are largely beyond the ability of national institutions to monitor, let alone control. Whilst the idea of the state apparatus having too powerful a say in precisely what is transferred and what is not, is not especially attractive, there is a legitimate fear that the processes are capable of being manipulated to a nation's disadvantage.

The organizations which are the most effective users of the transfer of data are the international corporations, whose size and power already presents such a challenge to national sovereignty. They are now able to obtain and pass on data in such quantities and at such speed that even the governments of large countries can scarcely hope to match their knowledge. These companies tend to have access to a greater range of up-to-date information on less developed countries than the governments of those countries themselves. This can include information on trading fluctuations, the discovery of natural resources, or other strategic concerns. Such information can signal catastrophe for the country, but only the need to relocate its assets to the transnational. On the other hand, it can suggest the opportunity for great profits and give the party that is in possession of the information a major advantage in negotiations.

A number of international agencies, in particular those associated with the United Nations, have taken a strong interest in information provision, which has usually involved the harnessing of the new information technologies for the benefit of developing countries. In several cases this has resulted in the design of international information systems, with perhaps the best known example being the Agricultural Research Information System (AGRIS) which was set up in 1975 by the United Nations Food and Agriculture Organization (FAO). It is in essence a decentralized bibliographic system for agricultural information which has been very effective in providing both on-line and conventionally published information. Although criticized on some grounds, for instance for the poor quality of its indexing, AGRIS has performed reasonably well in the developing countries of Africa as well as other regions. The main reason for this is that since countries are permitted to contribute their own bibliographic records to the system they are in a strong position to influence the content of the service. It is true that this influence is largely a relative one, since only 25 percent of AGRIS content is input by developing countries, but this is distinctively positive in a context where most bibliographic data bases are overwhelmingly dominated by the developed world.[26] As a consequence of this, not only is the content of AGRIS of relevance to Africa, but the participatory element of the AGRIS scheme has stimulated some local activity and assisted in the development of a locally-based information workforce.

Another example which demonstrates not only the problems of computer networking in Africa, but also what can be achieved within the continent, can be found in Mali with the Industry Council for Development (ICD) Sahel Information Network. The system was originally the brainchild of a Malian health technician, Magnan Diakite, who saw the potential for establishing a data base to collect health information. The system was subsequently expanded after the intervention of the United Nations and the ICD and now embraces not only Mali, but also Burkina Faso, Niger and Senegal. The scope of the system has been expanded to cover water, health and agriculture, and contains information stored in a central data base accessible from a number of remote IBM personal computers. The nature of the information held and the technology used to handle it are both described as proving appropriate to the particular needs of the region.[27]

The potential for such initiatives is enormous, with the major impediment being telecommunications. Such networks, if they are to be effective and give access to worldwide systems or other inter-African networks such as the Pan African Documentation and Information System (PADIS), need to rely on a telephone system superior to that presently existing in most of Africa. Telephone lines originally installed during the colonial period are showing their age, and refusing to work efficiently. The colonial powers were mainly interested in providing telephone links between the metropolitan country and its colonies. Linking one part of Africa with another was seen as highly unprofitable and perhaps even dangerous as the groundswell for independence grew. Thus north and south links are better developed than east and west links, with parallel systems being directed towards London and Paris.

What this means in practical terms is that it is easier to phone from Nairobi to London than it is from Nairobi to Mombasa which is in the same country, or from Nairobi to Dar es Salaam which is just next door. It means that to get a telephone line from Djibouti to Lesotho, it is necessary to go via operators in Paris, London and Johannesburg. The problem is to some extent being solved by satellite links which permit the countries which have acquired earth stations to communicate much more directly. This alone, however, does not completely resolve the difficulty, as generally speaking Africa's telephone system is still underdeveloped and holdups and misconnections are the norm. The telephone systems are certainly not adequate to enable the creation and use of effective inter-African and international information networks.

Despite these difficulties, there have been numerous attempts at developing regional information systems, the most talked about, yet possibly the least successful, being the Pan African Documentation and Information System (PADIS).[28] The PADIS programme began in 1980 and is administered by the United Nations Economic Commission for Africa (ECA), based in Addis Ababa. It has two broad aims. The first is to help African countries strengthen their own internal information systems by various means, including advice and training. The second is to set up a decentralized information network for the continent. The latter is to take input from national focal points and feed it into a computerized data base which will in turn produce not only bibliographical information but also statistics and referral information on African experts, institutions, and development projects. The main product from this system so far has been the publication of *Devindex Africa* which concerns itself strictly with development literature.

Despite the fact that *Devindex Africa* sets high standards of bibliographical production, and has a considerable polish in terms of its appearance, there are serious problems. The content shows a high level of reliance on published and semi-published materials from developed countries as well as information from the ECA or UN itself. The semi-published material (or 'grey literature') is difficult enough to obtain in Europe or North America, whence much of it originates, and the acquisition problem is magnified for distant and underfunded African institutions. Worse than this, however, is the evidence that at present the service is largely failing to meet the original objective of bringing together Africa's information about itself.

A recent consultancy by Wilson Aiyepeku[29] further suggests that the organization has a disturbing suspicion of and unwillingness to co-operate with other international agencies working on information in Africa. Aiyepeku is basically optimistic about PADIS, and makes a number of suggestions as to how its activities in Africa can be nurtured at a grassroots level. One is left, nevertheless, with the uneasy feeling that the system may already be overcommitted to an information technology which not only is inappropriate in terms of its application, but is also rendered partly redundant by PADIS's location in Addis Ababa. This capital cannot by any stretch of the imagination be described as being at the hub of inter-African communications and telecommunications. A simple letter from Southern Africa posted to Addis Ababa usually takes weeks to arrive, and presumably the West African postal system, with its notorious vagaries, could not improve on this.

This unease is increased when the mechanisms for feeding PADIS with information from the various sub-regions of Africa are examined. The situation is confused, to say the least, and seems to change at frequent intervals. In East and Southern Africa, for example, a sub-regional grouping named ESADIS (East and Southern Africa Development Information System) is supposed to provide input from the sub-region to a co-ordinating centre in Zambia. Unfortunately, the centre never seems to have functioned properly probably because "the equipment which was brought in to establish the regional centre has already become obsolete while it apparently lies, still not unpacked somewhere in the capital.''[30] Apparently the major disagreement centred around which institution should host the focal point and while this dispute raged on, the equipment which had been donated waited in the safe custody of the Zambian customs authorities.

ESADIS was not even alone in the region, for there was a similar initiative known as SADIS (Southern African Development Information System) which was supposed to have its headquarters in Zimbabwe, and in addition had links with the African Bibliographic Centre (ABC) based in Washington. For a time a publication known as *SADEX* was produced which, while it lasted, proved to be fairly useful at informing those interested in development in Southern Africa of what was happening in terms of projects, publications, and international co-operative efforts. Suddenly and without warning the publication vanished from the scene and not a word about SADIS or *SADEX* has ever been heard of since.

The will to discover an effective means of exploiting the information resources that exist within the region is quite apparent, and hopefully has not been destroyed by the hopeless confusion brought about by the variety of organizations, institutions and individuals involved, all apparently with their own contradictory and conflicting agendas. In May of 1986 yet another regional meeting was convened in Southern Africa to discuss 'Informatics for Development'. The venue was the Victoria Falls, Zimbabwe, and the meeting was heavily dominated by telecommunications and computer experts, with the resolutions mainly focusing on the technical arrangements necessary for information networking. One of the most interesting questions came from a Zambian librarian who had the temerity to ask just what PADIS was doing, how did it fit into the plethora of regional information systems that were apparently emerging from nowhere, and, more pertinently, who was supporting what?[31]

Satisfactory answers to such questions have, as yet, not emerged. All that one can say at this juncture is that the financial input into PADIS has been enormous. Its ten-year budget of $160 million is high by any standards[32] and the period since it was created is long enough for the question to be asked as to what has been achieved. The answer seems to be, pathetically little, despite the major proportion of the budget having gone into supporting a commitment to information technology. The question as to who, apart from the manufacturers of computer technology and the staff whom PADIS employs, has benefited from this effort raises even more serious doubts, for the products and services which one has reason to expect from an operation with this level of funding simply do not exist.

The reasons are not difficult to discern, and in many ways PADIS typifies much of what is going wrong when information technology is introduced into Africa. The strategy of PADIS, in attempting to link nations together by placing heavy reliance on information technology, seems very questionable, especially when the countries who are supposed to participate in the PADIS network possess a telecommunications and computer capability that at its best can only be described as unreliable and severely underdeveloped.

Many examples such as the ones cited above can be used to illustrate the case that technological solutions for the information needs of Africa are far from an easy recipe for success. Yet failure to adapt to the new information technologies could quite conceivably further marginalize Africa. The question is not whether information technology should be acquired, as the answer to this is 'Yes.' The major questions now should concern what use Africa wants to make of computers. How can they be used in such a way that they further the interests of Africa? How can computers be used in such a way that they do not further marginalize what is already a large majority of the population who cannot read or write or who have little access to the existing information products? How can computers be used to alleviate rather than exacerbate Africa's already chronic information famine?

Conclusion

Towards the beginning of this chapter, we posed the questions 'What do the people know?' and 'How do they know it?' Our answer has been that, in the first place, what they know is rooted in the ancient wisdom based on village communities and generations of accumulated knowledge. They know this principally from those who by custom and tradition act as the human repositories for what a particular community needs to know. There is, nevertheless, much information available through written documents of all kinds and there is beginning to be some information available via electronic technology.

It is because of the way in which Africa simultaneously presents the ancient and the modern, side by side and bound together, that information in the continent offers both more problems and more potential than it does in the much more predictable and systematized communication environments of the developed countries. This opening chapter has said very little about the specific problems of librarians. This is because of our conviction that libraries and, indeed, other information institutions, cannot be properly understood unless defined within the context of a broader information environment. In the next chapter, therefore, we shall consider not merely the information which Africa already has, but the additional information that it needs, in particular for national development. We shall also try to show how the nature of the information and the way in which it is transmitted influences the development process and affects the development of the continent. In the succeeding chapters, we shall attempt to show how the library, as it is found in Africa today, fits into that environment, and how best the library can relate to it in the future.

References

1. Crowder, M. The book crisis: Africa's other famine. *African Research and Documentation*, 41, 1986. 1–6.
2. Mwanza, F. Zambia—a nation bereft of good books. *The Chronicle* (Zimbabwe), August 5th, 1987. 9.
3. Unesco. *Statistical Year Book*. Paris, Unesco, 1986.
4. Ryan, M. AIDS: the frightening facts. *New African*, 220, 1986. 7–8.
5. Ive, O. Cameroon: crushing censorship. *New African*, 249, 1988. 39–40.
6. Anderson, H. *The participation of women in rural development: the case of Singida region.* (Unpublished monograph), 1985.
7. Vansina, J. *Oral tradition as history.* Madison, University of Wisconsin Press, 1985.
8. Hayward, F.M. A reassessment of the conventional wisdom about the informed public: national political information in Ghana. *American Political Science Review*, 70, 1976. 433–451.
9. Hayward, F.M. *op. cit.*
10. Cutter, C.H. Political communication in a pre-literate society: the example of rural Mali. *Rural Africana*, 27, 1975. 9–23.
11. Boafo, S.T.K. Utilizing development communication strategies in African societies. *Gazette, International Journal for Mass Communication Studies*, 35, 1985. 83–92.
12. Anon. Publish and perish. *New African*, 249, 1988. 35–40.
13. Nwuneli, O.E. International news coverage in Nigerian newspapers. *Gazette, International Journal of Mass Communication Studies*, 29, 1982. 31–40.
14. Newspapers for rural areas—a crying need. *Daily News* (Botswana), 141, 1988. 5.
15. Escarpit, R. *Trends in worldwide book development, 1970–1978.* Paris, Unesco, 1982.

16. Unesco. *An international survey of book production during the last decade.* Paris, Unesco, 1982. p 20.
17. Kotei, S.I.A. *The book today in Africa.* Paris, Unesco, 1981.
18. Obiechina, E. *An African popular literature: a study of Onitsha market pamphlets.* London, Cambridge University Press, 1973.
19. Oluwasanmi, E., McClean, E. *and* Zell, H. *eds. Publishing in Africa in the seventies.* Ife, University of Ife, 1975.
20. Obasi, J.U. Bibliographical control of Nigerian publications: social science primary materials. *Journal of Documentation*, 38, 1982. 107–124. p 115.
21. Msiska, A.W.C. Early attempts at creating African literature: its distribution, local authorship, and library service in Northern Rhodesia (Zambia) and Nyasaland (Malawi). *Libri*, 36, 1986. 240–246.
22. Osa, O. *Nigerian youth literature.* Benin, Paramount Publishers, 1987. p 14.
23. Lancaster, F.W. *The dissemination of scientific and technical information: towards a paperless society.* Champaign, University of Illinois, Graduate School of Library Science, 1977.
24. Kuitenbrouwer, F. The world data war. *New Scientist*, 91, (1269), 1981. 604–607.
25. Olden, A. Sub-Saharan Africa and the paperless society. *Journal of the American Society for Information Science*, 38, 1987. 298–304. p 299.
26. Samaha, E.K. Document delivery: the AGRIS cooperative solution. *Information Development*, 3, 1987. 103–107. p 103.
27. Mayo, E. Building up the deserts and forests of information. *The Guardian*, August 18th, 1988. 29.
28. Abate, D. *Libraries and information services in a changing world: the challenges African information services face at the end of the 1980s.* Paper presented at IFLA General Conference, Brighton, U.K. August, 1987.
29. Aiyepeku, W.O. *International socio-economic information systems: an evaluation of DEVSIS-type programs.* Ottawa, International Development Research Centre, 1983.
30. Lungu, C.M. Resource sharing and self-reliance in Southern Africa. *Information Development*, 3, 1987. 82–86. p 85.
31. *Ibid.*
32. Gehrke, U. Information for development. Some problems of national co-ordination, regional co-operation and international assistance. *INSPEL*, 9, 1985. 166–198.

Chapter Two

Information and Development

Introduction

More than twenty years ago, the economist Wolfgang Stolper, in his book *Planning Without Facts*,[1] made the dramatic allegation that the development of Nigeria was being attempted blindfold. No doubt the tourist or casual visitor, experiencing Lagos for the first time, or for that matter many Nigerians themselves, would not wish to argue with this assertion. What the author had in mind, though, was something more than the turmoil and chaos that is a major ingredient of everyday life in Nigeria. Stolper was employed as an adviser to the government of newly independent Nigeria, but unlike many who worked in a similar capacity, he admitted that very often the development planners had little notion as to what they were actually doing. In particular he mistrusted the bold and grandiose plans of his fellow advisers, because he could see that they were formulated on the basis of an extremely fragile and often threadbare information base.

It was not only the absence of statistical and demographic information that concerned him, but also the lack of facts on a much broader base which he felt were needed to produce plans that stood a chance of succeeding. Barely ten years after he wrote, Nigeria's agricultural production had fallen quite dramatically. Some of the major causes of this decline included the civil war, the discovery of oil, the impact of the Sahelian drought, and the general drift of people to the cities from the rural areas. However, Stolper had already demonstrated that the planning process was starved of the type of information that he believed would contribute to understanding the fundamental contributory elements for effective agriculture. For example, he pointed to the paucity of information that was available at the time on Nigeria's physical environment. He also drew attention to the importance of knowing about social structures, traditional culture and beliefs, patterns of land tenure, and all the other features related to the human circumstances of farming communities, which are likely to govern the acceptability or otherwise of a particular development project or community-based programme. Much subsequent planning had demonstrably not taken account of the specific geographical or human circumstances obtaining, and its failure was deducible from his principles. This detachment from the mundane realities of life in the places where development schemes were attempted could, perhaps, be attributed to arrogance on the part of planners, but it could just as convincingly be put down to ignorance.

Stolper's arguments still seem almost as relevant today. Africa is still characterized by inadequate demographic data collection procedures, a poor statistical base, and a general paucity of information about itself. Sadly, his ideas were largely ignored in the 1960s and forgotten in the 1970s, yet the problem he identified has not gone away. As recently as 1986, it could still be said that "Policy making therefore continues with an inadequate information base. The situation described by Stolper in *Planning Without Facts* still exists in virtually all sub-Saharan African countries."[2] What has become more obvious in the 1980s are the ways in which information can contribute to vital decisions that can bring either positive change or catastrophic consequences for the continent and its suffering people. It is how information relates to development that forms the theme for this chapter.

Development—the information dimension

During the 1950s and early 1960s, when much of the African continent achieved political independence from European colonial rule, it was fervently believed that independence would usher in a new era. The expectations of Africa and its leaders were high and almost certainly went beyond the narrow vision of mere self-government. Likewise, the mood of the populace at the time of independence in most of the newly-created states was one of strong optimism about the benefits which would accrue from the end of colonial rule. In view of the crisis in which virtually the whole of Africa found itself enmeshed during the 1970s and 1980s, this optimism may now seem to have been mistaken.

At the time of independence, the favourable prices which could be obtained for the agricultural products and minerals which formed the staple exports of most African economies provided comparatively substantial currency reserves. Bold development strategies were conceived and set in motion, and swift expansion of education, health care and infrastructure were the expressions of the newly-won independence. Yet unfortunately Africa's progress over the succeeding period has not fulfilled the earlier expectations, to the extent that Africa in the 1980s is now regarded universally as a continent in crisis. As to what went wrong, it may be useful to briefly consider, as examples, the development strategies that were adopted in relation to agriculture and industry.

Some nations, most notably Tanzania, saw their future in terms of an emphasis on farming and on a gradualist policy towards the introduction of technological change. The policy was succinctly expressed by Julius Nyerere, when he stated that "The jembe [hoe] will have to be eliminated by the ox plough before the latter can be eliminated by the tractor".[3] This, however, represented a minority view, and much more common in most African countries was a faith in an industrialization strategy. For many political leaders and development planners, agriculture was regarded as a backward sector, producing 'colonial' crops, which were vulnerable to price fluctuations and which represented a visible sign of dependence. Any inputs into the agricultural sector would only be made in order that it could contribute better to the surpluses that were necessary to finance industrial development.

Industrialization was seen as capable of ensuring a high rate of economic growth, bringing greater economic independence and the means to finance the social and infrastructural development necessary after many years of colonial neglect. This was a view propagated by numerous economic advisers, regardless of their political persuasion. For instance, A.F. Ewing, who acted as an adviser to the United Nations Economic Commission for Africa in the 1960s, argued that "industry is the sole means of raising the productivity of an economy".[4] Paul Baran, a Marxist economist, adopted a similar standpoint, arguing that farmers "could be provided with opportunities for productive work only by transfer to industry".[5]

This type of prescription can now be seen as a disaster, with the industries that were created often operating at only minimum capacity or falling into disuse. Meanwhile the agricultural sector has suffered such neglect that Africa is now compelled to import food in order to feed its people. The nature of this neglect has been comprehensive, and the following generalizations about policy apply to much of the continent. In addition to minimal government investment in agriculture (receiving over the years about 5 percent of annual government expenditure), credit allocations have tended to favour industry over agriculture, prices of agricultural products have been artificially held down with the aim of providing cheap food for Africa's growing urban population, and market conditions have been distorted to the disadvantage of farmers via control of exchange rates and tariff structures.

Changing external circumstances should also not be neglected as contributing to Africa's development problems. World economic recession caused African commodity prices first to fluctuate and then to fall dramatically. An economy heavily dependent on a single export, like Ghana with its cocoa, was devastated by such a trend. The oil price rise in the early 1970s was a second major blow, contributing to stagnation and decline in economies that had little alternative but to rely on imported oil. Drought throughout the Sahel, the Horn of Africa, and the south of the continent threatened whole regions with desertification and practically destroyed domestic food production. As domestic output shrank, so the price of imported foodstuffs and other manufactured products steadily rose, to an extent that Africa was unable to pay for their purchase. Governments turned to deficit financing after discovering that abundant credit was easily available on the world financial markets, particularly from Western banks. For the moment, anyway, a disaster had been averted.

The 1980s, however, witnessed substantial rises in interest rates, so that servicing the debt that had been incurred during the previous decade became impossibly expensive. Vast amounts of capital and foreign currency reserves were being expended on payment of this debt, which meant in turn that little remained to finance new agricultural projects that could have helped to alleviate some of Africa's more persistent problems. This conjunction of unfavourable external circumstances and disastrous internal policies has been largely responsible for Africa's current crisis, but nevertheless only partly explains what went wrong. There has been no lack of people willing to offer explanations. Books, journal articles, research and consultancy reports, academic dissertations, and even programmes on television, have been produced in profusion, each with its own explanation as to what the problem is, and each offering a different solution. It is not our intention to further examine Africa's economic crisis, or to add to this type of material. Our primary concern is with information, particularly its role in Africa's development and its potential contribution to the process of development planning.

Apart from the arguments put forward by Stolper more than twenty years ago, the relationship between development and information has rarely been given serious discussion. Africa's poor economic performance has usually been attributed to the humiliation of colonialism, the burden of underdevelopment, the legacy of dependence, the negative impact of an alien Western culture, and the internal turmoil of a continent in transition. A considerable body of literature now exists to support such views. Information is only one of the ingredients that will help solve Africa's development problems. Nevertheless, it can be argued that it is an important ingredient, and one that until fairly recently has been neglected in the discussion. It is for these reasons that we wish to resurrect the points Stolper made over two decades ago, and to see how applicable they are today.

The scope of any discussion on development in Africa is bound to be wide ranging, embracing a complex of topics including industry, agriculture, transport, health, education, natural resources, social services, and nutrition. It should be sufficient to highlight two, agriculture and small scale industry, in order to illustrate the point that the lack of a sound information base has been one of the common features in much of Africa's policy making.

Agriculture

After the obvious failures of large scale industrialization which tended to mar the post-independence phase, many economists and development planners began to focus their attention much more on agriculture and rural development.[6] This was not entirely for the first time, for as early as the 1950s the colonial administration in many parts of Anglophone Africa had attempted to mobilize local communities through an approach known as 'Community Development'. The main emphasis of this type of programme centred around encouraging rural communities to work together to construct facilities such as bridges, schools and clinics. The approach was not successful for a variety of different reasons, the principal one being that the local organizers did not know how to integrate community development projects into the social, cultural, economic and agricultural structure of the local community.

Although some countries still continued to follow such an approach, the favoured system in the 1970s was known as 'Integrated Rural Development'. This involved a concentration of efforts on some major project or projects, usually administered by a variety of semi-autonomous agencies. Examples were the Action Priority Zones Programme in Cameroon, the Lilongwe Land Development Programme in Malawi and the Special Rural Development Programme in Kenya. The majority of these programmes have subsequently been criticized for the inappropriate matching of proposed technical changes to small farm conditions. According to Uma Lele, whose detailed work provides the chief published source on this topic,[7] what was lacking was an insufficient knowledge of, and sensitivity to, local institutional patterns. What was required to make many of these projects successful was a systematic acquisition and use of local knowledge. This seldom formed part of Integrated Rural Development programmes, and the spectacle of development experts wringing their hands over failed projects, and bemoaning the fact that Africa was somehow different, was a common occurrence.

The 1980s heralded a greater recognition that much of the difficulty in project implementation does not necessarily rest with Africa's rural farmers. Rather, it arose from development planners who attempted to impose projects on local communities without any serious attempt at gaining an understanding as to how those communities worked and functioned. As a result, the emphasis in agricultural development has shifted to 'Farming Systems Research' which has been developed from the premises that:

a. previous work has failed to take the information needs of small farmers into account;
b. there was a gap between the education, values, and interests of researchers and extension workers on the one hand, and farmers on the other;
c. studies had often considered too small a sample;
d. the impact of social and political institutions on household decision making has been neglected;
e. research findings were seldom disseminated in a form usable by the farmers.

Farming Systems Research attempts to reverse these failures by developing "Research programmes which are holistic, inter-disciplinary and cost effective in generating technology which is appropriate to the production and consumption of rural households in specific micro-environments".[8] During the last decade more than half the countries of Africa have initiated research programmes of this type. They have been able to draw on work from other disciplines such as cultural anthropology, whose practitioners, unlike economists and development planners, have always been more concerned with societies as they were and as they are, rather than as they should be.[9]

The shift towards research as a basis for rural development planning has naturally led to a need to improve the collection and processing of information. This in turn has resulted in attempts to improve the quality of service required to disseminate this information. Usually the first, often the only, and thus the most widely-used type of service available to carry out both these functions has been agricultural extension. Agricultural extension is the type of service designed to bring government into contact with the rural populace through the agency of fieldworkers, who both communicate information to the farmers and collect feedback at the same time. Unfortunately extension service has proved to be far from ideal for a number of reasons.

It has been argued that "Substantial domestic and external resources have been devoted to the creation of sizeable agricultural extension programmes which have generally been quite ineffective because they have had so little to extend."[10] This refers back partly to the problem of research, but also to the lack of communication between organizations, as well as the general non-availability of information in a form that could be readily used by extension workers or farmers. There is in addition a consistent vein of criticism concerning the structure and organization of the services themselves. They tend to rely on a large staff of para-professionals, whose morale is often undermined by poor and irregular pay, as well as inadequate training and supervision. The information that the extension workers are supposed to disseminate too frequently takes the form of a series of highly technical packages, which are no doubt as incomprehensible to them as they are to the barely literate farmers they are struggling to advise.

In addition, the extension worker is supposed to collect information, in particular statistics on crop production and other farming activities, which in theory is then supposed to be fed back to the researchers, thus completing a neat cycle of communication. This does not always work out, often because of the suspicion that can naturally attach to any government agent collecting information. One function of extension workers involves the supply of inputs such as seed, fertilizer, and herbicides, usually from state monopoly agencies. Quite naturally, if there should seem to be any threat that the supply of such inputs is going to be reduced because of the extension workers' information-gathering activities, then the rural farmer will try to ensure that the activity of gathering the information is made as difficult as it possibly can be. It is for reasons such as these that Africa's agricultural extension services, though widespread and well-established, are generally ineffective as a means of collecting and disseminating information, a process which supposedly lies at the heart of Farming Systems Research Programmes.

Small scale industry

In a similar way, the problems inherent in Africa's small scale industrial sector tend to support the argument that the inadequacy of the knowledge base is one of the factors that is retarding development. Governments' initial concentration on large industrial projects generally led them to ignore and neglect the informal industrial sector, where individuals, many of whom possessed few skills and a limited educational background, were often establishing and profiting from a variety of business activities. Economic advisers were either uninterested in this phenomenon or were unaware that considerable volumes of economic activity, possibly accounting for as much as two thirds of Africa's total industrial employment, were taking place, regardless of the development planners' preference for large scale projects.

Part of the difficulty in coming to terms with small scale industry is that it relates to a phenomenon that has proved hard for economists and planners to conceptualize. This is the phenomenon of migration. All over the continent people have for two or three generations been leaving their rural homes for work, or the prospect of work, in the towns. This can mean mining, farming or domestic service in South Africa, or less predictable opportunities in fast-growing metropolises such as Lagos or Kinshasa. It leaves the rural areas mainly populated by women, old people and children, largely dependent on remittances from the towns. More visibly, it creates the enormous and chaotic shanty towns and self-help areas that surround the centres of cities. Warfare and drought have compounded the process that ambition began. The migrants largely exist outside the ability of government to count or tax them, let alone provide them with services and facilities.

The scope of their industries is consequently insufficiently known and their patterns of organization little understood. The remaining rural population is also perceived as having a need for sources of income such as can be provided by small scale industry, to supplement the unreliable proceeds of agriculture and remittances from migrant family members. Governments often look to rural industrial schemes as a way of stabilizing population levels in rural areas. Clothing production and wood- and metalworking are the chief types of small scale industry, with food production (usually baking and brewing) and repair trades also very common. The majority of small firms employ only a handful of people, while many are one-person enterprises. As yet too little is known about this sector, but one of the earliest surveys in Lome, Togo,[11] not only testified to the abilities of this sector to create employment, but also, perhaps surprisingly, to the resource-fulness, adaptability, efficiency, and even the self-financing capacity of these business communities.

Where government has sought to assist, its attempts have not been particularly successful. Kenya, for example, has offered credit facilities, via the Industrial and Commercial Development Corporation, and has established industrial estates through Kenya Industrial Estates Ltd., as well as a number of Rural Industrial Development Centres. Most centres have offices, classrooms and workshops which act as a base for extension activities to businesses scattered in small communities. The major criticisms have focused on the inability of the centres to attract sufficient users to justify the expensive equipment maintained in the workshops, as well as the poor response to the extension service.[12]

Quite obviously this picture has strong similarities to that in agricultural development, with the sector eluding attempts to either control or assist it. While the problems associated with small scale industries are many and varied, they have so far rarely been considered as being information-related. However, information does quite clearly play an important part, not only in terms of its ability to solve the day-to-day problems of these small scale entrepreneurs, but more importantly in terms of its potential contribution to technology transfer and the diffusion of innovations. This is the process whereby established technology is acquired by one firm from another, whether by purchase under licence, by imitation, even piracy, or from publications or numerous other types of information resources. The burgeoning industries of Asian countries like Japan, South Korea and Taiwan gained considerable benefit from such an approach, to the extent that they are now able to produce cheaper and better products that are highly competitive in the world market. Africa, by comparison, has not been able to follow this successful lead, and while as with agriculture it is often the continent and its people that are blamed for such deficiencies, it could well be argued that the problem is one that concerns the process of technology transfer, and in particular the role of information in that process.

While there is a wealth of research and publications produced on the effects of the transfer of technology to developing countries, very little has been said about the complex processes by which information about new ideas, products and processes is acquired, absorbed and put to practical use. In particular, the role of what are referred to as 'non-market-mediated' means of transfer, including, amongst other things, the use of publications and the media, as well as library and information services, has been insufficiently examined. Instead, discussion has tended to assume the availability of technical information from one source or another, and has then moved directly on to examine the effects of this knowledge when used by the firms which have acquired it.

Fortunately, there has of late been a growing realization that much more emphasis needs to be placed on the information component of any technological transfer or, for that matter, any small scale industrial project. The Botswana mud oven training course[13] illustrates this point, as well as highlighting the complex process that can be involved when introducing technical change to an embryonic small scale industry. The training was intended to introduce a technique whereby women could bake bread which they would then be able to sell in order to supplement their meagre subsistence livelihood. The technique was a proven one, and women, who already had experience in preparing and selling food for the local market, were able to benefit from it. However, in cases where that prior experience was absent, and no background information was provided to compensate for the lack, the women failed to derive any useful benefit from the technology.

Technology transfer, then, can be seen as an information problem. Quite clearly, though, no given technology can be transferred in its entirety, however complete the accompanying blueprints, instruction manuals, and associated expertise. What cannot be transferred is the local knowledge that has contributed to its original success, since such packages of documentation and expertise cannot be expected to contain relevant knowledge of the new locale. This local knowledge consists of information on markets, both for raw materials and finished products, on the availability of skills to work with the new technology and maintain it, on tariffs, subsidies and loans, and on the various social and cultural nuances that can have such an important effect on whether a change is accepted or not. Some of this information is, in theory, the type of thing that government agencies should be able to provide, but other aspects are difficult for those outside the immediate locality to acquire and tend not to be available in neat, pre-processed packages. The art is to draw together a mix of official information and the very local knowledge that the small business community already has at its fingertips to introduce the new technology in a way that will be conducive to its successful adoption.

Yet the perceived need for technical information that would boost small and medium scale industry, and the actual reality, are often in conflict. The point cannot be better illustrated than by quoting at length the findings of a Unesco expert who visited Tanzania on a mission to conduct a field study of the application of technical information to development. His investigations focused on two factories, one for sisal and the other for kenaf, both of which were installed with Italian participation. He recounts that:

> The sisal factory was completed in 1968/69 with an initial cost of 55 to 60 million shillings and the kenaf factory in 1972 with a cost of more than 20 million. Instruction manuals for the operation and maintenance of the machines were furnished in Italian. As a result the local engineers and technicians were unable to read them and could not maintain the machines as required. Moreover they could not even work the machines efficiently or order spare parts when the necessity arose. For the last couple of years the situation in the sisal factory is dramatic. Some machines are out of order and the others are working below capacity or producing too much waste. The losses are very heavy and Texco has requested the assistance of a foreign expert for a diagnostic study . . . The kenaf factory has encountered fewer problems because the machines are not so old and the processing of kenaf is an easier operation. For maintenance purposes they have succeeded in finding someone in the region who knows enough Italian to assist them in reading the manuals. According to the manager and his senior technicians there is little need for information other than that required for maintenance. However they will be interested to purchase more books and magazines, if they are provided with a list of relevant titles. It appears that no one in the factory knows how to get this information.[14]

An obvious question is 'Whatever happened to the Tanzania Library Service?' Even if they could not have found information on translators, they were surely in a position to provide bibliographical assistance. This is a question of a kind that we will look at in the next chapter. For the moment it is sufficient to conclude by re-emphasizing the point that different sectors of the economy are quite clearly bedevilled by a lack of an appreciation of the value and utility of information. This deficiency is embodied in many aspects of the acquisition, absorption and dissemination of information, but what is most typical is that it often revolves around ignorance on the part of those who wield the power, make the decisions, and control the financial resources. Even in the few instances where there is such an awareness, albeit somewhat vague, it is rarely translated into a practical programme of information acquisition and use. A major reason for this is general ignorance as to whom to turn to when information is required. Although there are libraries with relevant services, for instance in agriculture, there is little perception that they could perhaps be of some help.

The World Bank and the Organization of African Unity

Having attempted to expose some of the extent of the information problem in two sectors of development, it would now be useful to see how far a perception of it has reached the economic and social planners who are attempting to develop the entire continent. In 1981 the World Bank produced a report, *Accelerated Development in Sub-Saharan Africa*,[15] which was heralded by many development planners and policy makers, mainly based outside the continent, as the seminal document on development in Africa, and was even, according to one commentator, perceived as ''a new source of revealed wisdom through a secular variant on the Book of Revelation''.[16] Unfortunately, four years later, in 1985, the actions proposed in the report had not been initiated. A former president of the World Bank, Robert McNamara, commented on the state of Africa at that time as follows:

> The harsh truth is that sub-Saharan Africa today faces a crisis of unprecedented proportions. The physical environment is deteriorating. Per capita production of food grains is falling. Population growth rates are the highest in the world and rising. National economies are in disarray. And international assistance in real terms is moving sharply downwards.[17]

Prior to this, in 1980, the Organization of African Unity (OAU) had produced its own strategy document, *The Lagos Plan of Action*,[18] which presented prescriptions for Africa's ills largely based on the principles of co-operation between African states. Although its recommendations were warmly embraced by many African governments, it proved to be as unsuccessful in its implementation as the World Bank report, and has as yet had little impact on Africa's development crisis. The volume of criticism and counter-criticism the reports have engendered has been more or less in inverse ratio to their practical effect. However, there is a positive significance in terms of the approaches which they both take towards information issues. In fact it would not be an exaggeration to claim that more than twenty years after Stolper first raised his voice, the two reports have at last placed information firmly on the development agenda.

The World Bank report was prepared after an extensive information gathering and data collection exercise which enabled it to pass judgement, not only on the inadequacies of the data that were available but also on the extent to which information that was available was not being effectively used in the planning process. Specific mention was made of the need for more information on topics such as rainfall, river flows, soil quality, farming systems, and patterns of land use, as well as the need to bring information more closely to bear on public sector decision-making.

The Lagos Plan, by comparison, seemingly placed far less reliance on the information-gathering process in reaching its conclusions, and has in some quarters been criticized for its lack of empirical data. Yet, paradoxically, what it has to say about information is much more important. For instance on agriculture it concludes that research findings need to be made available without delay to the farming community. It accordingly recommends a closer link between research and extension services and greater emphasis on the spread of proven technologies. The section dealing with industry similarly contains two elements which have a strong information significance. First, as a contribution to economic co-operation, it calls for the exchange of information among African states on the technical and financial specification of projects, and the creation of institutions to make an inventory of shared national resources. Existing institutions which could be seen as potentially significant in information terms, such as the African Regional Centre for Technology, and the African Regional Centre for Engineering Design and Manufacturing, are accordingly recommended for strengthening. The problem of technology transfer is also considered, with a call, in particular, for the free availability of inventions, patents, and technical know-how to form the basis for an African technical information service.

Information on natural resources is very strongly identified as a basic need. Acknowledgement is made of the fact that African countries do not have a full knowledge of their natural resource endowment, and what is more, that much of the knowledge that does exist is in the hands of transnational corporations. A series of specific proposals are made in response to this, including governments asserting control over the results and basic data (maps, films, logs, etc.) arising from prospecting by transnational corporations. National surveying and mapping institutions are recommended for strengthening, as well as the creation of national documentation centres to ensure the best possible storage and use of data, including geological documentation, reports, maps and surveys.

The section of the report dealing with science and technology is quite explicit on the potential contribution of information, pointing out that ''lack of information is one of the most serious obstacles to selection, acquisition, and use of appropriate technology options. An understanding of the local environment, character and orientation of the transferees is as important as information on the technology to be supplied''.[19] It proceeds to recommend the establishment or strengthening of national technology information centres, liaison between such centres on a regional level, including PADIS, and the undertaking of studies on agricultural and industrial extension services, so as to obtain improved feedback on their effectiveness.

As has been previously pointed out, throughout much of the past decade, the debate on Africa's development has been centred on these two sets of proposals—the Organization of African Unity's *Lagos Plan of Action*, and the World Bank's *Accelerated Development*. Much of the debate has been acrimonious and confrontational, with both reports managing to produce an impressive array of supporters and detractors generating a broad spectrum of arguments expressing either approval or dissent. While the reports differed markedly in terms of how they perceived Africa's development crisis, and in the prescription they offered to solve it, the one consensus that did seem to emerge was that concerning information. By even discussing information, both reports introduced a new dimension to the debate on how Africa should develop. Both seemed to agree that at the present time, planning and development in Africa is being carried out on an imperfect knowledge base. Both seemed to agree that knowledge creation, information generation and data collection should receive more emphasis, if policy and development decisions were to be improved. Unfortunately, while both reports acknowledged the new and enhanced role that information should play in Africa's development, neither of them had really concrete proposals as to how this could be achieved, or a full appreciation of the problems involved. It is to the information resources that are required to service Africa's development that we must now turn our attention.

Information resources for development

Africa's need for development information is something we believe has been amply proven. There are clearly discernible signs of an appreciation of the importance of information in the development process, as evidenced above. The next logical step, therefore, is to establish whether the required information exists, and if so, what its particular characteristics are. This last point is important, for the distinctive character of information, the media which convey it, and the institutions which handle it, will appreciably alter the value attached to it and ultimately the meaning derived from it. While development planners obviously use a wide range of information resources, an examination of the creation and use of statistical data should be sufficient to illustrate and develop this point.

In 1987, Peg Clement, who was working as an Information Co-ordinator in Maputo for the development and relief agency, CARE, brought Africa's statistical difficulties to life when she recorded the following conversation[20] which took place at a rehabilitation centre for drought victims:

"How many people live in this rehabilitation centre?"
"Oh, many, *many*."
"About how many would you say, just roughly more or less?"
"There are so many, very many."
"And where are they coming from? Which districts are they coming from?"
(Pointing) "Over there, very far."
"To the south you mean?"
"S-o-o far away."
(Trying a different tactic) "There seem to be many hundreds of people here."
(Suddenly . . .) "Two thousand, senhora. We have this information. Two thousand."
"Two thousand *people* or two thousand *families*!?"
"Fam . . . no, people, maybe, individuals." (A factor of five is at stake here)
(A colleague interrupts) "No, it's families." "Two thousand people." (Firmly)

It is such occurrences which provide confirmation of the notorious problems associated with Africa's statistical data. The major difficulty is that there is a shortage of published statistical material from most African countries. Censuses of population are wildly inaccurate and are rarely carried out at regular intervals, and even then, according to Clement, "Rounding-off numbers for convenience's sake is a real culprit in the number-chase game. Hundreds of people appear or disappear at whim."[21] Then there is the problem that the statistical material that has been published suffers from serious flaws which results in misleading and inaccurate data. The problem was dramatically revealed in the report of the 1977 meeting of the Conference of African Statisticians which stated that

> Quantity estimates of gross agricultural output include a significant amount of guess work owing to the lack of available statistics, even for basic commodities. Food crop estimates are sometimes based on eye estimates by field agents. For some countries estimates of food crops are based on a variety of sources, such as data on population, and estimates of per-capita consumption from fragmentary and sporadic household surveys, or information on acreages and yields.[22]

The problems associated with statistics are, of course, universal. It is quite common for governments in countries like Britain or America to announce that figures which have been issued month after month, and year after year, on some crucial matter such as volumes of imports and exports, have all along been wrong. The problem may have been a faulty computer program or the incorrect recording of some seemingly minor element. If this is not uncommon in countries with old-established, well-funded statistical services, staffed by large numbers of highly qualified and experienced people, it is hardly surprising that the services of developing Africa also make mistakes. There are however, problems peculiar to the continent which cause the situation to be quite serious.

In the first place there is the fundamental problem that the original material collected in the field is likely to be less accurate than its initial appearance may suggest. A large part of this can be attributed to the fact that the statistical techniques available are, for the most part, a product of the industrialized nations of the northern hemisphere. They thus embody assumptions which may not be applicable in the developing countries of Africa. In the collection of crop statistics, for instance, the assumption that farmers will be able or even willing to express the areas they have under cultivation, in metric units, is likely to be unrealistic. Another assumption based on European practice is the expectation that farmers will sow a single crop, which can be registered in the statistics as being cultivated on a particular area of land. This fails to recognize that African farmers get better yields on certain types of land by double-cropping, and therefore cannot give figures that easily fit the statisticians' categories.

Secondly, the collector of statistics is often faced with a number of intractable problems, caused primarily by an inappropriate set of questions, arising from the importation of a basic set of inapplicable assumptions. The field workers themselves have been characterized as "under-trained, lonely, under-supervised, over-worked, ignorant, bored, underpaid strangers, who may be forced into corruption, including collusion with respondents who have rightly persuaded them of the futility of their task".[23] The respondents themselves are likely to react with suspicion and incomprehension to the intrusion that the field worker presents, particularly if there is the possibility that the information they are asked to provide will lead to decisions that may have dire consequences for their continued well-being and livelihood.

At the next stage, there is the problem of the processing to which the original material collected in the field is subjected. This can be carried out with the best and the worst of intentions. There seems to be almost a blind faith amongst statisticians that the more sophisticated the processing to which the raw data is subjected, the more authentic and useful will be the results. As a consequence, more reliance is placed on the value of particular sets of figures, perhaps processed by computer, than their original content merits.

There are also clear indications that in many cases the resulting data, if not ignored, are massaged, manipulated, distorted and mis-represented in an attempt to make them seem to illustrate trends that conform to the requirements of those who wield power, whether it be a government, a multinational corporation or even an international development agency. The saga of Sudan's 'vanishing famine' illustrates the kind of dispute which can underlie the production of figures that are subsequently presented to the world as authoritative evidence for some phenomenon or other.

In 1986, during the avalanche of news coverage of the Ethiopian famine, a consortium of up to sixty aid agencies which were working in southern Sudan announced that as many as 2 million Sudanese faced starvation by the end of the year. But a contrary opinion, debunking the whole notion of a famine in the south, was consistently voiced by a Reuters News Agency reporter who was trapped in Wau during the months of August and September. He even, in one article, quoted an anonymous aid official who stated that the figure of 2 million was pure fiction. Relief agencies continued to confirm that a full-scale famine of Ethiopian proportions was taking root in the south. At the same time individual relief workers familiar with the locale denied such grim pronouncements, although they did say that much of what was going on was a severe development problem. The confusion was further compounded in November when Prime Minister Mahdi, who was fighting a civil war in the south, informed *Newsweek* magazine that the figure of 2 million was totally untrue. To further confuse the case, he then proceeded, at a news conference in Rome during December, to talk of a food surplus and the possibility of exporting food to people in worse situations.[24]

It is impossible at this stage to know just how reliable the figure of 2 million was. Clearly the conflicting reports, the denials, the affirmations, as to the numbers actually starving, led many to question whether there actually was a famine in southern Sudan. Reporters, government officials, and aid organizations argued over the numbers, confirming or denying the figure of 2 million. With the best will in the world, the situation of southern Sudan made it particularly hard to produce reliable figures. In the heat of this debate the parties concerned committed their reputations to particular versions of the truth to the extent that subsequent collection and publication of accurate statistics was rendered even more difficult. Meanwhile as the debate went on, the uncertainty as to whether there really was a famine both slowed and limited the kind of relief effort that could have done something for those (however many) who were actually dying of starvation.

Finally, there is the problem of what is done with the statistics that have emerged from this doubtful process. Some, at least, of the results are published, very often in summary form and often without a great deal of supporting commentary. They are then available for all kinds of uses, such as the framing of specific development plans. It is only occasionally that a reference can be found which casts doubt on the reliability of these statistics. For example, the United Nations *Demographic Yearbook* (1981) did highlight some of the problems, including the common practice of borrowing data "from a neighbouring country where conditions are assumed to be similar".[25] In the main, however, public debate amongst development economists and planners on the accuracy of these figures seems to be avoided as much as possible. This is no doubt because of the understandable fear that confidence in the whole process of development planning would be seriously damaged if the statistics on which it is based were exposed as unsound.

It is not, therefore, merely a question of Africa's development crisis being resolved through the use of more and more information, which some commentators, including the majority of the library profession, would have us believe. What is required is something far more basic and fundamental, and that is the improvement of the quality of Africa's knowledge base. Even this would not guarantee the success of the planning process, for perfect statistics do not guarantee perfect plans. They would certainly improve the prospects, however, and at the very least ensure that there was less of an excuse when things did go wrong.

We must not forget Stolper's observation that statistical data represent only part of the information resources that can contribute to solving Africa's development crisis. Geographical, ecological, historical, legal and cultural information all contribute to the required knowledge base. Research on many African topics is worth pursuing, not only for its own intrinsic interest, but also its potential practical value. Such research, though, is of little use if its results are not available to those who could use them. With this in mind, we will now examine the difficult circumstances that have to be endured in obtaining access to research results.

Access to information for development

Africa's libraries are, almost without exception, the last places that the serious researcher would visit in order to find information concerning Africa. Although this assertion will be explored in more detail in the following chapter, suffice it to say that very few libraries can yet boast a comprehensive and current Africana collection. The question is, now that information is at last making an appearance on Africa's development agenda, accompanied by the realization that the quality of information has to be dramatically improved, will the finished product be readily available to those who require it? There is no reason to assume that the situation in the entire continent is any different from that in Ghana, where "There is awareness of the need for data in planning for every establishment in the nation. The main problem is the difficulty of getting the required data, and the lukewarm attitude of some establishments towards the acquisition of data".[26]

In the first place, the way in which such important information is often published does not make it easy for African institutions to acquire it. Nothing illustrates this point better than the case of the *Lagos Plan* itself. The plan first circulated in mimeographed form from the offices of the Economic Commission for Africa (ECA) in Addis Ababa, and was despatched to each African government. This clearly failed to make it readily available, to the extent that an American economist producing a copy of the plan at a conference in Kenya in 1983 was overwhelmed by African colleagues, eager to see the document for the first time.[27] To compound the indignity, when a final version of the plan did eventually appear it had been printed in Switzerland. It is undoubtedly a tragedy that a document of this importance should have been treated in this way, and highly ironic that its elusive pages say so much about improving Africa's information capacity.

Another major reason why research results are hard to obtain is that those responsible for the research, as well as those on whose behalf it is carried out, disregard a nation's legitimate need to accumulate knowledge about itself. For example, at a recent gathering in Nairobi, over 200 of Africa's leading scientists from 40 countries complained that their research efforts, which are producing results that in many instances have global implications, are being frustrated by their own governments' disregard. Professor Samson Gombe, secretary of the African Academy of Science, cited a recent example from Kenya, "where a special lamp was designed to detect inferior coffee berries before processing, an important function for high-quality blends and one that is hard to perform by eye alone".[28] Because of the lack of interest from the Kenyan coffee industry, as well as the absence of any effective form of legislation to protect research and intellectual property, the lamp was patented in Europe, and could soon be re-exported back to Kenya, after considerable loss of face and foreign exchange.

A considerable amount of research information is generated by the activities of multinational companies. In many instances this is of crucial economic importance. For example, international mining companies, because of their wealth and technical capacity, can exert enormous control over natural resource and geological information, to the extent that the host country may not be in a position to know exactly how much is being mined. The activities of Consolidated Diamond Mines (CDM), De Beers' Namibian subsidiary, dramatically illustrate the point. As a result of the Thirion Commission investigation into corruption in the Bantustan governments in Namibia, CDM was damningly indicted for overmining and for misleading local officials. The company was accused of a deliberate

attempt to exhaust the country's diamond mines before independence, distorting crucial information concerning not only the quantity
and quality of gemstones being extracted, but also the size of deposits
still left in the ground.[29]

The paradox is that legitimate research in many African countries
can only be conducted after permission has been granted either from a
national research body charged with such a mandate, or at times even
from the office of the nation's Head of State. To some extent, this is
perhaps not unreasonable. Certainly in the past, research in Africa
has often meant little more than the continent being used as some type
of exotic laboratory. It has not been uncommon for research projects,
sponsored by outside bodies, and usually dominated by foreign
researchers, to have published their results in a way that could be seen
as distorting or denigrating Africa and its people. Suspicions of this
kind have led African countries to seek to improve their control over
what is researched by whom. This emphasis on control is naturally
unpopular with potential researchers, but, even worse, it has diverted
attention from the vital issue of establishing effective mechanisms to
ensure that the final product of research is suitably published and
made easily accessible to those who might use it.

The question of suitable publication is extremely important. The
vast majority of research material produced on Africa can be identified as belonging to a distinct category of information resource that
has sometimes been referred to as ephemera, fugitive, non-
conventional, informal, or—the more generally accepted term—grey
literature. In addition to research and consultancy reports, this type of
material can be made up of a variety of items which are not available
through the normal publication channels, and includes reports, min-
utes of meetings, data collections, conference papers, reprints, theses,
technical rules, and so on.[30] The material, although not formally published and marketed for sale, does have more than temporary significance, and represents a vast potential store of knowledge about Africa.

A study of grey literature in Lesotho,[31] based on the acquisitions of
the documentation centre of the Institute of Southern African Studies,
at Roma, has revealed a considerable amount of detail about this type
of material. In a three year period of intensive collecting effort, the
institute managed to acquire just under 3,000 documents, including
180 (often rather irregular) annuals and more than 100 periodicals.
These figures are worthy of note, for Lesotho is a very small country,
and the facilities and resources available to the institute are far from
lavish. A proportionate volume and a similar effort from larger and

better-endowed countries would no doubt confirm that grey literature forms a very bulky category of documentation, as well as one with a very significant content. Indeed estimates that grey literature represents something like 70 percent of the publishing in Nigeria, or 60 percent of publishing in Africa,[32] very probably underestimate the proportion by a sizeable factor.

The situation in Lesotho is, however, rather better than that in many other countries. The comments of the economist Balabkins illustrate the problems any researcher can face when trying to access this type of material. Most grey literature is thought to be inaccessible because nobody, including most librarians, pays much attention to it. Quite the opposite can be the case, as these comments show:

> Nigerian military government officials particularly hoarded the grey literature. This practice served to increase their power vis-a-vis other groups in society, and, to judge by the complaints of the Nigerian and expatriate business community about the difficulty of obtaining information, it did so effectively. The practice also served to increase the income of officials, for they did make the grey literature available in exchange for bribes.[33]

This renders a large part of discussions of acquisitions and bibliographical control distinctly marginal. The majority of African countries do have a national bibliography, which does generally succeed in listing the bulk of the conventional output of the country. However, when it is considered that some countries like Burundi, Djibouti or Somalia, are considered by the Library of Congress's East African Field Office in Nairobi to have virtually no commercial publishing sector at all, and that even Nigeria, the giant of African publishing, lists an average of only about 1,000 titles a year, the significance of conventionally published literature is placed in better proportion to the more numerous grey sector.

The virtual absence of grey literature, not only from Africa's national bibliographies, but also from her library shelves, is an issue that has been insufficiently discussed by librarians. They have tended to avert their gaze from it because it is obviously difficult to cope with, and have been able to justify themselves because it does not fall within the traditional scope of the librarian's task. Fortunately, other institutions, in particular archives, which have a strong proprietary interest in information at this embryonic stage, are taking up the challenge. Archives are too frequently regarded as guardians of historical material, which might be of interest to the academic researcher, or have some value to the nation's educational system, but which has no relevance to more urgent issues related to national development. This, however, is far from being the case, and the National Archives of Zimbabwe, for example, has an explicit policy "to intensify its efforts to encourage the maximum use of semi-current records by government officials".[34] This is based on the conviction that a considerable amount of archival information can be used for national development planning purposes.

Semi-published reports of the grey literature kind consistently form part of archival holdings, and are particularly useful in this context. Statistical information is a major example of material that can be acquired from archival sources. The Zanzibar Archives, which began taking in records from the Ministry of Agriculture in the early 1980s, encouraged use by advisers working on the decline of clove and coconut production and possible diversification. "The agricultural advisers, initially sceptical, were delighted to find that once the files were processed and stored in the Archives they could quickly retrieve information on the coir fibre industry, cocoa planting, citrus fruits, or chillies. British and German aid officers working on clove and coconut research were also enthusiastic about the accessibility of past investigations and trials. Moreover the Zanzibar government was now in a position to link the planning of any new agricultural development initiative to past policy and its results, while aid officers working in Zanzibar in the future would be able to assess the background to the Ministry's operations".[35]

The challenge of providing a comprehensive collection of grey literature which not only has the depth of coverage to respond to the shifts in priorities and interest of researchers, but is also easily accessible to those who need to use it, is one that Africa's librarians need to face. In response, Kay Raseroka, Librarian of the University of Botswana, has suggested a re-arrangement of priorities, with the acquisition of local material, in particular grey literature, being given central importance for the collections of most libraries.[36] The short-term implications of such a policy shift would be very hard to accept for many librarians who are used to regarding the output of the most famous international publishers as their standard of excellence. Such is the importance of the capture of this material, however, and so great the need to make it available, that Africa's librarians have little choice in the matter.

The final main issue in relation to the problems of access to information concerns information from outside the nation's boundaries. The acquisition of books and journals from other countries, chiefly North

America and Britain, has been much discussed in the literature, and will feature prominently in the next chapter. A tone of despair is the usual feature of such discussion, with the high and increasing expense of the materials being contrasted first with the overstretched acquisitions budgets of African institutions, and then with the limited or often non-existent amounts of foreign currency that governments are able to make available for book buying. The situation has become so critical that "Many Nigerian authors published abroad cannot have their books read at home due to resrictions on importation: the singular instance is Wole Soyinka's *Ake* published four years ago in London, enthusiastically reviewed all over the world, yet not one copy of which is available in any bookstore in his own country".[37] If this is what can happen to the works of an acclaimed international author such as Soyinka, what hope is there for the considerable body of knowledge on Africa that lies outside the continent?

The study of Africa by the rest of the world can be characterized as having passed through a number of distinct phases. It started with the logs and diaries of the early explorers, was codified and bureaucratized by colonial administrations, provided with an evangelical persuasion by the missionaries, became academically fashionable during the 1960s, and has endured through the 1970s and 1980s. As a result there has emerged a considerable number of universities and organizations outside the continent, particularly in North America, Britain, France and West Germany, which have a specialist interest in Africa.

In Britain, for example, there exists a network of universities which contributes to the research and study of Africa. It includes specialist centres at Birmingham which deals with West Africa, and at York, which specializes in Southern Africa. In addition, many other universities employ individual Africanists dispersed throughout faculties and departments who serve as foci for this network. Other bodies concerned with the study of Africa include the British Library, the Africa Centre, the International African Institute, and the African Studies Association. A similar situation exists in most other countries of the Western world, as well as in the Soviet bloc countries and to a much lesser extent in parts of the southern hemisphere. For example, in North America, the twenty-seventh annual African Studies Association conference held in 1984 attracted over 1,000 participants and heard more than 300 papers which were discussed in at least 100 panels, many taking place simultaneously.

The result of all of the interest which Africa has generated, especially over the last couple of centuries, is a considerable accumulation of documentation. While this represents a valuable store of knowledge, it is nonetheless problematical not only in terms of access, but also because of the circumstances under which it is now being used. Although figures for the volume of research on Africa, conducted outside the continent, are elusive, estimates indicate that more than 8,000 theses on Africa are available from University Microfilms International (UMI), with more than 80 percent having been produced since the 1970s. This has been discussed by Alexander Robertson, who adds that:

> Organisations like UMI provide a vital service by making much completed work accessible, but it is plain that the vast bulk of research conducted in Africa has been effectively lost in that it is not reasonably accessible to other students. It may be, for various reasons, incomplete, or it may be lying unreferenced in any one of a thousand small colleges or research institutions. Meanwhile an American student, say, proceeds in ignorance not only of the Swedish student who is pursuing the same issue, but also four other students who are writing or have just written their theses.[38]

If research on Africa is not accessible within and between developed countries, which can boast highly sophisticated techniques for retrieving information, then one can safely say that the bulk of research on Africa, done outside the continent, is totally inaccessible to Africa. As has been noted by Richard Rathbone[39] of London University, what is even more disheartening is the fact that, over the last five years or so, some of the best African scholarship can be seen to have emerged from African scholars on attachments to, or in collaboration with, foreign universities or research institutions. Unfortunately, the bulk of this material, even when produced in published form, is generally not available within Africa, mainly because of the poverty of the continent's libraries.

Perhaps what is even more disturbing is that the knowledge base supporting the study of Africa from outside the continent is now rapidly diminishing in terms both of the amount of material that is available, and of its quality and currency. Just as it is exceedingly difficult for the researcher working within Africa to acquire primary source material, so is it fast becoming wellnigh impossible for the researcher based outside the continent. The problem of acquisition of African materials is not only causing Africa's library collections to be inadequate, but is also leading to a decline in the rate of growth of those library collections outside Africa which over many decades have attempted to cover the continent. In addition, and what is perhaps more alarming, the corps of scholars and researchers based outside the continent who are termed Africanists, are themselves now part of the problem of Africa's diminishing knowledge base. They belong either to the greying and rapidly diminishing generation who emerged as a result of the growth of African studies in the 1960s, and whose experience of the continent was during the first flush of independence, or to the younger generation, who have had no comparable experience and little opportunity to benefit from direct contact with Africa or to conduct field investigations there. This younger generation's study and research is dependent almost entirely on library collections whose quality is diminishing.

This in many ways completes a cycle of famine which results in everyone, especially Africans themselves, knowing less and less about Africa. The cycle starts within the continent itself with planners, decision makers, development planners, researchers and scholars being, in one way or another, denied access to the information they require. The problem is then further compounded by the numbers of Africans who receive their postgraduate education overseas. The research they carry out while overseas is almost entirely dependent on the available reources, both human and bibliographical, in the host institution. As has been previously noted, such resources are becoming less truly representative of Africa's knowledge base. Incomplete though the final product must be, the African scholarship that takes place outside the continent is frequently of considerable merit. Unfortunately, Africa seldom benefits from this effort, as most of the resulting research material will either only be available outside the continent, or on the bookshelves of the returning scholars' houses.

Information technology has recently become relevant to African studies, and although as yet there is little evidence that it is contributing any solutions, its arrival has helped to give a sharper focus to the problems. Much has already been said in the previous chapter about the introduction of information technology into Africa. What has not been discussed so far in any great detail is the proliferation of data bases on Africa which are located outside the continent. Although as yet there is no single comprehensive data base dealing with Africa, there are a growing number which either consider the continent in terms of a specific subject or sub-region, or adopt a multidisciplinary approach. Accurate figures as to the number of data bases of direct concern to Africa are not available, though it has been estimated that it could well be in the region of 700.[40] It would be useful to discuss three examples of these, two of which, FRANCIS and InfoTrac, are general data bases, and the other, SACDT, specifically African in content. They are not only part of the solution but also possible contributors to the problem.

According to a recent account,[41] the FRANCIS data file, which is a general data base produced by the French Centre National de la Recherche Scientifique, contains 1,000,000 items and inputs 90,000 new items per year, including much about Africa. It includes research from all over the world, on a broad range of subjects from ethnology through to administrative science. It is available on-line from anywhere in the world, and aims to be easy to use by non-French speaking countries. InfoTrac is an on-line periodicals index developed and marketed by the Information Access Company (IAC), of Belmont, California. It is very user-friendly by design, and can provide printouts of citations for readers in a matter of seconds without the assistance of a librarian.[42] InfoTrac is user-friendly, not only because of the technology it employs but also because the journals that it indexes are particularly accessible ones. SACDT, which is a text data base on Southern Africa, based at the Centre of African Studies, University of Liverpool, is perhaps the most interesting example. Established in 1985, it aims to use an IBM mainframe (3083) computer to create a Southern African data base of primary information drawn from various media resources, chiefly newspapers. The director of the project has reported that the system so far contains information on various aspects of South Africa's efforts to destabilize the region, the economic, political, and military situation within the region, and its relationships with the outside world.[43]

Different from each other as these three examples are, they do share the same problems. These can be defined as access, input, and availability. Enough has already been said in the previous chapter on the vagaries and weaknesses of Africa's communications networks and telecommunications systems to cast serious doubt on the ability of any of these data bases to provide on-line assistance for the researcher who, for example, is based in Somalia. True, there is potential for the exploitation of off-line searches or selective dissemination of information services, which could use the postal system to transfer the information from the data bases to users for whom on-line is an unrealistic option. There is, however, no evidence of really determined attempts to use the technically less demanding options to provide service from data bases to African users. What seems to be the best option of all is the use of data bases on optical disc, in particular CD-ROM (Compact Disc-Read Only Memory). An increasing number of important data bases are being offered in CD-ROM versions and experimentation with their use in African countries is well advanced.[44] It is still an expensive, vulnerable technology, but it has the enormous virtue that it is not dependent on telecommunications links.

Even when the problems of access from Africa have been resolved, the researcher will then no doubt be surprised how few of the resulting citations are derived from material produced in Africa. FRANCIS for example, as of March 1986, contained over 36,000 items of African relevance. These were dominated by articles from journals, comprising 86 percent of the total. Of these, 60 percent were published in Western Europe, 7 percent in Eastern Europe, and less than 1 percent in Africa. Meagre though this sounds, it may represent quite a high proportion of what could conceivably have been gathered. Yet even if the quantity of material published in Africa to be found on a general data base like this can be considered quite creditable, it still represents less than an ideal bibliographical service for the continent. Little has been published so far about the actual make-up of the SACDT file, but in view of the virtual absence of bibliographical control over Africa's newspaper output and the serious problems that are experienced in acquiring copies of newspapers and periodicals, what is on the data base will have been put there after considerable difficulties have been overcome.

Finally, with the exception of examples like SACDT, which is a textual data base, most data bases provide only a list of bibliographical citations. Very often they give little assistance in locating the material. While data bases such as InfoTrac have concentrated on indexing accessible journals, the question 'Accessible where?' is the important one. 'Not in quite a few parts of Africa' may be the answer, with Makerere University, Uganda, as an example. Here, according to Michael Crowder "the existing holdings had to be defended with barbed wire because the Librarian and his colleagues found pages of scientific journals being used to wrap groundnuts in the local market. Library attendants had sold off the books for the value of the paper to supplement their abysmally low wages".[44] Any listing of material which could be obtained from a data base would only increase the frustrations of academics and researchers working in such conditions.

Conclusion

At the beginning of this chapter we argued that the whole development exercise was conceived and carried out in ignorance, and that the consequences of this have contributed to the failure of many policies, programmes and projects. This ignorance was most significant at the decision-making level, and it is quite clear that what often led to misconceived and frequently disastrous planning decisions was not simply ignorance of things to which no answers had as yet been found, but a failure to find out and learn from those who actually had answers.

The reasons why relevant information seems to have had little influence on development planning are not too difficult to discern. Most obvious is the absence or inadequacy of information systems which could have placed the relevant documentation on the desks of those who needed it. There was and still is enormous scope for libraries, in particular, to make a contribution to more effective national development. They can do this just by making sure that the decision makers get the chance to see information that can help them make sound and informed decisions. The fact that Africa's libraries are not doing this, even after nearly three decades of independence, will be the focus of our attention in the next chapter.

References

1. Stolper, W.F. *Planning without facts: lessons in resource allocation from Nigeria's development.* Cambridge, Mass., Harvard University Press, 1966.
2. Spenser, D.S.C. Agricultural research. *In*: Berg, R.J. *and* Whitaker, J.S., *eds. Strategies for African Development.* Berkeley, University of California Press, 1986. p 226.
3. Nyerere, J.K. *Freedom and Socialism.* Dar es Salaam and London, Oxford University Press, 1965. p 320.
4. Ewing, A.F. *Industry in Africa.* London, Oxford University Press, 1968. p 11.
5. Baran, P.A. On the political economy of backwardness. *Manchester School of Economic and Social Studies,* 20, 1952. 66–84.
6. Eicher, C.K. *and* Baker, D.C. *Research on Agricultural development in sub-Saharan Africa: a critical survey.* East Lansing, Department of Agricultural Economics, Michigan State University, 1982. (MSU International Development Paper 1.)
7. Lele, U. *Design of rural development: lessons from Africa.* Baltimore, Johns Hopkins University Press, 1975.

8. Eicher, C.K. *and* Baker, D.C. *op. cit.* p 159.
9. Seddon, D., *ed. Relations of production: Marxist approaches to economic anthropology.* London, Cass, 1978.
10. Johnston, B.F. Strategies for agricultural development. *In*: Berg, R.J. *and* Whitaker, J.S. *op. cit.* p 166.
11. Demol, E. *and others.* Lome's informal industrial sector. *In*: Fransman, M., *ed. Industry and accumulation in Africa.* London, Heinemann, 1982. pp 354-371.
12. Livingstone, I. Alternative approaches to small industry promotion. *In*: Fransman, M. *ed. op. cit.* pp 354-371.
13. Liedholm, C. *and* Mead, D.C. Small scale industry. *In*: Berg, R.J. *and* Whitaker, J.S., *op. cit.* 308-330.
14. Samaha, H.A. *A study of the application of scientific and technological information in development. Field study in Tanzania.* Paris, Unesco, 1978.
15. World Bank. *Accelerated Development in sub-Saharan Africa: an agenda for action.* Washington, D.C., World Bank, 1981.
16. Green, R.H. *and* Allison, C. The World Bank's agenda for accelerated development: dialectics, doubts and dialogues. *In*: Ravenhill, J. *ed. Africa in economic crisis.* London, Macmillan, 1986. p 61.
17. McNamara, R.S. *The challenge for sub-Saharan Africa.* Sir John Crawford Memorial Lecture, 1st November, 1985. Washington, D.C., World Bank, 1985. pp 31-32.
18. Organisation of African Unity. *Lagos Plan of Action for the Economic Development of Africa, 1980-2000.* Geneva, International Institute for Labour Studies, 1981.
19. *Ibid.*
20. Clement, P. The numbers game. *New African*, 241, 1987. p 18.
21. *Ibid.*
22. *Quoted from* Africa: a statistical profile. *In*: *Africa Report*, 28, 1983. p 58.
23. Hill, P. *Development economics on trial: the anthropological case for a prosecution.* Cambridge, Cambridge University Press, 1986. p 33.
24. Clark, C.S. The vanishing famine. *Africa Report*, 32, 1987. 68-70.
25. *Quoted from*: Africa: a statistical profile. *op.cit.*
26. Akam, A.A. Information system for planning in Ghana. *Planning and Administration*, 9, 1982. p 114.
27. Browne, R.S. *The Lagos Plan of Action versus the Berg Report.* Laurenceville, Va., Brunswick Publishing Co., 1984. p 29.
28. Matheson, A. African scientists thwarted at home. *Observer*, August 28th, 1988. 27.
29. Toolis, K. SA report damns De Beers. *New African*, 224, 1986. 58.
30. Balabkins, N.W. Collecting information in a developing country. *Harvard Library Bulletin*, 32, 1984. p 67.
31. Ambrose, D. Collection and bibliographic control of grey literature of Lesotho. *African Research and Documentation*, 36, 1984. 11-24.
32. Obasi, J. Bibliographical control of Nigerian publications: social science primary materials. *Journal of Documentation*, 38, 1982. 107-124.
33. Balabkins, N.W., *op. cit.*
34. Kamba, A.S. Archives and national development in the Third World. *Information Development.* 3, 1987. 108-113.

35. Thurston, A. The Zanzibar Archives Project. *Information Development*, 2, 1986. 223–226.
36. Raseroka, K.H. Relevant library services in developing countries. *IFLA Journal*, 12, 1986. 288–291.
37. Irele, A. An African perspective of publishing for African studies. *In*: Sternberg, I. *and* Larby, P.M., *eds. African Studies. Papers presented at a colloquium at the British Library, 7–9 January, 1985.* London, The British Library, 1986. p 84.
38. Robertson, A.F. Perspectives on African studies in the United Kingdom: the social sciences. *In*: Sternberg, I. *and* Larby, P.M., *eds. op. cit.* p 19.
39. Rathbone, R.J.A.R. Perspectives on African studies in the United Kingdom: history and politics. *In*: Sternberg, I. *and* Larby, P.M., *eds. op.cit.* p 27.
40. Seeley, J. The use of bibliographic databases in African studies. *African Research and Documention*, 41, 1986. 7–12.
41. Rahard, M. and Bourdin, J.F. FRANCIS can inform you on Africa. *African Research and Documentation*, 42, 1985. 8–19.
42. Easterbrook, D.L. INFOTRAC and Africa. *African Research and Documentation*, 44, 1987. p 12.
43. Munslow, B. *and* Pycroft, C. The Southern African Computerised Data/Text (SACDT) System. *African Research and Documentation*, 45, 1988. 9–14.
44. Kinney, J. Agricultural information services and the new technology. *In*: Asamani, J.O. *and others eds. Libraries and Literacy. Proceedings of the Seventh Meeting of the Standing Conference of Eastern, Central and Southern African Librarians, Gaborone, 4–8 Aug 1986.* Gaborone, Botswana Library Association, 1987. 23–33.
45. Crowder, M. The book crisis: Africa's other famine. *African Research and Documentation*, 41, 1986. p 5.

Chapter Three

The Imprint of the West

Libraries and dependence

The fortunes of Africa over the period since independence have not fulfilled early hopes. While it is no longer fashionable to blame every present misfortune on the colonial past, it is nevertheless true that the entire continent is still firmly tied to that past in a way that is not always beneficial to its people. A dependent posture can be witnessed in the complex of political, economic, social and cultural relationships that have endured since independence. Libraries represent only a tiny fragment of the mosaic of relationships that exist between Africa and the outside world, but they do provide a good example of the persistence of the colonial heritage and the stultifying effects of the dependent relationship that exists between Africa and the West. It is the underlying characteristics of this dependence that will form the focus of this chapter.

Unfortunately, dependence is the term that best describes the state of library and information work in Africa. Libraries and other formal information systems have not featured significantly in the life of sub-Saharan Africa in the past, and modern times have done little to alter this. This is not to say that libraries or literacy did not exist in sub-Saharan Africa prior to the colonial period or independence. Indigenous alphabets were certainly in evidence, particularly in West Africa, but literacy in them seems to have been severely restricted. What is more, there is little evidence that the writings produced in these scripts were systematically preserved, circulated or organized for widespread use.[1]

One of the earliest libraries in Africa was one of the most famous libraries that has ever existed; the ancient library of Alexandria, in Egypt. Yet all early African libraries were confined to the northernmost part of Africa, and all seem to have been the result of Greek, Roman and Arabic influences on the Mediterranean fringes of the continent. Prior to the era of independence, some libraries were established, which were either of Islamic provenance, and thus dedicated to religious purposes,[2] or were of European origin, and usually racially exclusive.[3] Africa itself, despite the glories of rich and ancient kingdoms such as Ghana, Mali and Songhai, where learning and scholarship flourished,[4] has never had a library tradition of its own.

This began to change during the era of Africa's political independence. For some time previously there had arrived on the scene a small band of expatriates who were to set the course of library development in Africa during the crucial first years of independence. Evidence of their sojourn can be traced throughout East, West, and Southern Africa in the form of the library structures and the library tradition that are still in place today. This is the case, not only in the former British colonies and protectorates, which took their first lessons in librarianship from a metropolitan country with a highly developed library tradition but also in the countries which had been under the rule of France and other European colonial nations. The latter, although they had old and strong traditions of scholarly librarianship, had distinctly underdeveloped library and information institutions for popular education and leisure.[5]

Many of the pioneer librarians were expatriates who showed a far-sighted perception of what the problems of establishing libraries in economically developing countries would be. They clearly intended to develop systems and services that would be properly integrated with the social and political circumstances of their host communities.[6] Many of them were not only aware of the need to tailor library systems to the characteristics and aspirations of a newly independent Africa, but also recognized both the cultural diversity of the continent and the need to develop services that would accommodate the shifting patterns of a transitional era.[7] Their intentions were undoubtedly of the very best.

Yet it is not unusual for good intentions to go amiss, and this is what happened in these formative years of modern African librarianship. The legacy that the pioneers left failed to meet the objectives they had set themselves. What actually emerged from the early days were systems which reflected practice in the metropolitan countries. In most cases, the expatriate librarians probably had little choice.

Having recently arrived in their adoptive countries they usually faced the exigencies of planning an entirely new system, or occasionally reviving and strengthening embryonic institutions. No blueprints existed to assist them and their employers had little time for tentative or experimental beginnings.[8]

While the library mission to Africa was certainly well intentioned, it was also guided by a cautious pragmatism, rather than the results of any deep philosophical debate. This is perhaps not too surprising, for if one looks at what the British library profession was talking about in the earlier part of the twentieth century one tends to find a preference for discussing the minutiae of routine and rather less concern with examining the broader issues. American librarianship, which was such an important source of ideas and inspiration, was likewise suffering a period of disenchantment with the public library ideal. Michael Harris has described this as follows:

> Discouraged on the one hand by their inability to increase library use significantly, and on the other by their seeming failure to elevate those who did use the library, American public libraries began slowly, almost imperceptibly, to abandon their mission as originally defined by the founders. They were less and less able to provide reasons for processes that were being performed in their libraries, and they began to define 'functions' such as 'recreational reading' or 'informational service' as ends in themselves. They had lost their way, most had completely lost sight of the founders' vision, and the few who could still see it had lost their faith in its potential for fulfillment.[9]

Since much of what was being provided in African countries in the early days was new public library services, this stagnation of the Anglo-American library tradition was highly significant. Indeed, it is doubtful if the Anglo-American tradition was really in a fit condition for export to Africa.

Exported it definitely was, however, and the advent of independence did witness a remarkable quantitative expansion of library services. Much of this early effort was concerned with the establishment of structures and the creation of patterns of bureaucracy. There does not seem to have been the time available for discussion as to what Africa's own particular information needs were, and whether new solutions could be found to meet them. Isolated cases where noticeably different solutions were tried were few, and their outcomes were not necessarily happy ones. In Uganda, for instance, the period 1964–66 saw an attempt to provide a large number of library service points around the country as rapidly as possible. These were linked to an unusually informal central organization and involved a minimum of elaboration in the treatment of library materials. Problems associated with this fairly radical preference for immediately maximizing the impact of service to the community, as opposed to steady concentration on the established procedures for collection building, led to its early abandonment and the replacement of the then director. The Ugandan library service after 1966 prided itself on having a headquarters with full processing facilities, a proper catalogue, and a formal reference service. A 'real' library system had been restored and a hectic experiment with a different approach abandoned. [10]

During this early phase of library development in Africa, international organizations, charitable foundations and national aid or cultural agencies played a significant part. The work of such organizations as Unesco, the British Council, the Ford Foundation, the Carnegie Corporation, the Ranfurly Library Service and the International Federation of Library Associations (IFLA) has been extensively documented, and the contribution they have made to library development in Africa has received its due acknowledgement. In particular, Stephen Parker's review of Unesco's role in developing countries provides an excellent account, [11] while Beverly Brewster has charted the history of America's contribution between the years 1940 and 1970. [12]

Until recently, accounts of the British contribution to overseas library development could only be found in dissertations and theses. [13] Recently, however, this literature has been augmented by Douglas Coombs, whose book tells the story of the British Council's library work. He recounts how ''Since its birth in 1934 the British Council has been instrumental in creating a unique international library network, and has laid the foundations, at least in part, of many public library systems in the developing world'' and, more importantly, how ''The men and women who have worked as Council librarians overseas have, like missionaries, spread the word of their faith in a strong and free public library service as a powerful weapon in the struggle against ignorance, poverty and tyranny.'' [14]

Much of what has been written concerning the role of international agencies in library development has been from the perspective of the donor. Apart from recent work by Anthony Olden, now of Ealing College of Higher Education, on the beneficiaries of library policy in the ex-British colonies of Africa, [15] there has been no real attempt to offset this deficiency by conducting a thorough audit and preparing a comprehensive balance sheet to see who has actually benefited. By looking at some of the inputs which Africa's libraries have received we hope to show how donor priorities have shaped African library and information systems. Indeed, we feel that it is arguable that if the main prerequisite for the successful creation of library systems is awareness of the needs of the user, then African library work has often seemed to skip this step and to begin a little way further along the road.

Africa as a continent had, even prior to independence, a rapidly growing population with a desperate thirst for knowledge and educational advancement which the formal system of schooling could never satisfy. This is a situation magnified in the decades since independence and one surely ripe for response from the library and information professions. It was not surprising, therefore, that newly-independent Africa seemed to accept the public library idea with ease and remarkable speed. For instance, despite competition with other obvious and pressing concerns, legislation was enacted in many African countries soon after independence, committing governments to providing a free public library service. This was an extraordinary achievement when one considers that the same principle had only been won by the British and American library movements after considerable effort had been expended.

The African public, however, had not been consulted when schemes such as the British Council's Public Library Development Scheme were put into operation. Indeed our knowledge of the needs, and even the composition of Africa's potential library clientele is still largely based on conjecture and supposition. The people's verdict on new library systems was not long in coming, and has stubbornly endured to this day. Their response to libraries has, all too frequently, been one of scepticism and apathy. To the majority of Africans, libraries have appeared to have very little to offer.

Librarians, in turn, wring their hands in anguish, and lament the disinclination of the public at large to accept the obvious benefits obtainable from libraries. Since Africa's governments have lost their early enthusiasm for library services, in part at least as a consequence of this public indifference, librarians have resorted to exhorting each other to convince the decision makers of the importance of libraries. This touching faith in the power of reasoning in the absence of supporting evidence has, unsurprisingly, been of little avail. The reality is that after more than three decades of independence, and despite an initial enthusiasm, libraries are, at best, grudgingly tolerated by governments, and are placed low on any national list of priorities. If lack of relevance to users' needs is truly the source of this disillusion-ment, as we would argue that it is, then it is important to understand just how the services that are provided manifest the problem.

The architecture

The library, from the earliest times and throughout the world, has been perceived as potentially a monument to national, civic or institutional pride. It would be churlish to complain about the architectural mag-nificence and luxurious furnishing of the world's great national, research and public libraries and it is encouraging that many develop-ing countries have cared enough about their own libraries to seek something of the same style. This has, however, come to seem like overbuilding when the collections and services fail to match the pretensions of the building. No one should complain that African library systems seek to acquire the most impressive buildings that they can. Only if that conflicts with a pressing need for more numerous service points, stocked with more and better information resources, staffed with more and better educated personnel, and used by greater numbers of the public, is there cause to question the building policy. In a context of scarce resources it is arguable that a large number of simple service points, whether they be public libraries, reading rooms, special libraries or school libraries, are indeed better value for money than a comparatively small number of architectural gems. Plain but serviceable units, scattered throughout the country and built with the best local techniques and materials, would be a more effective symbol of the importance of libraries than imposing buildings largely con-fined, of necessity, to the cities. By this criterion quite a proportion of African library building begins to seem over-ambitious.

What is more, the architects responsible for designing African library buildings have often been been provided with a brief which takes too little account of climatic and other constraints on building in the continent. These architects, whether foreign consultants, who might not have always been fully aware of these constraints, or local practitioners with overseas professional training, have been respon-sible for some attractive buildings which have not responded well to the demands placed on them. A discreet veil is generally drawn over failures in library design and few have been documented, but their existence should, nevertheless, not be doubted.

For example, hot weather causes much distress to readers and staff, as well as exacerbating conservation difficulties. Air-conditioning is the solution which springs most readily to the architect's mind, and in some cases buildings which are almost wholly dependent on artificial air cooling and circulation have been designed and put up. In the context of electricity supply systems which are both expensive and unreliable and maintenance services hampered by shortage of spare parts and skilled personnel, a building using air-conditioning is highly vulnerable. When there are well-established building traditions in hot countries which make the best use of natural air circulation, it would not be realistic to ignore them, even if air-conditioning were more to be relied upon than it is.

Despite the suggestion that librarians, in preparing architects' briefs, may sometimes have paid too little attention to climatic constraints on library planning and design in Africa, it is true that at least one writer has elevated this to a central place in his philosophy. This is Wilfred Plumbe, whose early experience in the hot and humid parts of West Africa led him to identify climate as the major factor to be considered.[16] Important though climate is, our own emphasis would be much more on the necessity for building to be appropriate to a whole range of social, budgetary and geographical conditions. We would maintain that a realistic view of library building is a major element in the breaking free from dependence on imported versions of librarianship.

The collection

Empty library shelves are not an uncommon sight in Africa, particularly in school and public libraries. This is only sometimes due to the demands of an eager book-reading public. More often it arises from the simple fact that the library possesses very few books in the first place. A building and a librarian's salary may remain, even where a book budget has totally disappeared. When such depths have been reached, the effort required to secure the financial provision that would fill the shelves begins to seem impossibly great. It becomes easier for the librarian to carry on with an empty daily routine, whilst trying to ignore the fact that no books and no readers is likely, one day, to mean no job.

Where reasonably substantial collections do exist some of them are distressingly little used. This can have much to do with the unsatisfactory nature of their content and the view of the world which it represents. The African viewpoint is too little represented, and views from Europe, North America, and sometimes Russia and other socialist states, are usually much easier to obtain from the books on the shelves. The reasons for this are various. Africa's meagre contribution to the world's body of published knowledge, and the poverty of bibliographical information available on the continent's documentary record are major causes, and have already been addressed in previous chapters.

The African librarian's deep respect for the published output of the major international publishing houses should also be taken into account. This has meant that such funds as are available tend to be spent on material which represents either alien or deceptively 'universal' viewpoints. The late Sam Kotei, Professor of Library Studies at the University of Botswana, liked to draw scornful attention to the irrelevance of much of the expensive Western material that could be found in African libraries, often citing *Grove's Dictionary of Music and Musicians*, as his example.[17] This kind of acquisition is very much in the tradition of British or American libraries, which strive to "provide access to the whole of literature within the law of the land".[18] This principle has taken root in Africa and influenced acquisition policies, even though financial limitations alone make it quite unrealistic. Indeed it is doubtful if this ideal can be realized, in terms of acquisitions, by even the more richly endowed American or European library services. To find, as one of the present writers did, a recently purchased and obviously unread copy of a book on the Severn bore (a phenomenon by which tidal pressure causes the British river Severn to flow in the wrong direction at regular intervals) on the shelves of a remote public library in a country where drought has for years prevented water flowing in any direction at all in the dry river beds, is the sort of rich irony that arises from this attitude.

The inappropriateness of Africa's library collections is contributed to by the gifts and donations of charitable organizations and foreign governments and their agencies. The role of aid in perpetuating library dependence is a substantial one and needs to be looked at in some detail. As Mary Maack, of the Graduate Library School at the University of California, Los Angeles, points out in an excellent treatment of the consequences of aid for libraries, inappropriate donations can make a library grow without actually developing.[19] Library materials donated by governments are more likely to reflect the priorities of the donors than those of the recipients. American agencies have tended to give books that support the philosophy of free enterprise capitalism. This can be frustrating, or even have its slightly ludicrous side, as when the donation includes multiple copies of a popular explo-ration of the American ethos such as *I'm Allright You're Allright*. On the other hand, the approach of members of the Soviet Embassy bearing yet more duplicate copies of commentaries on the works of Marx and Lenin is enough to chill the heart of any African librarian. Language imperialism can play a part in this process too. Whilst it tends to be unspoken in Anglo-American terms, the French explicitly regard their library aid as a means of spreading their language, whatever the content of the books. They not only follow this policy in their former colonial possessions, but also have impressive libraries in other countries of the continent, particularly in the ex-colonies of Spain and Portugal, where French influence has reached the point where they treat some of the smaller countries almost as part of the *francophonie*.

While government donations are often too propagandist, gifts from charitable agencies often consist of the discarded miscellanea of libraries, publishers' remainders, or well-thumbed second hand volumes from well meaning philanthropists. For any librarian who has worked in Africa and has been on the receiving end of such unsolicited 'gifts' the experience recounted by John Harris when he was involved with the setting up of the library at Ibadan University will no doubt bring back painful memories. Soon after arriving at Ibadan, Harris received a bulky consignment of seventy large wooden crates, enough to occupy the entire space of a large room, which was the gift of a number of philanthropic organizations based in Britain, who had heard that Nigeria needed books. The collection was over 7,000 strong. In anticipation new shelving was erected to accommodate it, and hundreds of man-hours were spent unloading and sorting it. Yet at the end of the day it was discovered that over 90 percent was unusable. To add insult to injury, Harris was then faced with the problem of how to dispose of this collection of dirty, grimy texts which he described as follows:

> There were works on sanitary engineering designed for England in the nineteenth century; there were two volumes of a five volume work on the topography of Wales in 1820; there were books of essays on long dead ecclesiastical issues of Victorian England; there were twelve copies of Morley's *Life of Cobden*, and, possibly the least useful of the whole col-lection, twenty five copies of a pamphlet on How to Win the War, addressed to the Polish people, and in the Polish language.[20]

Harris fortunately had the good sense to dump most of these books, but what he described still reflects the current situation, and not all of

Africa's librarians have followed his lead in discarding the material. This is perhaps because of the attitude that some books are better than no books, but also because of bureaucratic constraints within particular institutions that make the discarding of material, no matter how useless, wellnigh impossible.

Examples of recent initiatives include The Brothers Foundation, based in New York, which is proving to be of considerable assistance to the American publishing industry by shipping remainders and out-of-date texts to Africa. This is far less expensive for publishers than incurring warehouse charges and provides welcome tax relief. The Ranfurly Library Service has in the past been a major provider of discarded and secondhand books to the less developed countries. Of late Ranfurly has launched a new Textbooks for Africa Project (TAP) which it is envisaged will be much more effective than its previous efforts. The initial responses from some of Africa's libraries, in particular in Malawi and Tanzania, are positive. The arguments for the continuation of such efforts are convincing, when set against a reality where a majority of Africa's children are growing up in a totally bookless environment.[21] Nevertheless one commentator has injected the correct note of warning into the argument:

> Obsolete books, though abundant, can tax scarce resources at every point. In Africa I have seen rooms full of unusable books. Graciously received, and displayed during official visits, they consume needed accommodation and other resources. Gifts of fewer, selected, especially requested, up-to-date books and journals can be a godsend.[22]

Despite the good intentions of most of these agencies, such donations can be positively detrimental not only to Africa's library collections, but also to the development of the continent's own indigenous knowledge base, book trade and publishing industry. Whilst we would certainly not wish to condemn all book donations out of hand, aid to develop the book industries of a country is potentially a great deal more useful. It can quite quickly make a very valuable contribution to the development of libraries by providing locally-published material for them to acquire. Existing schemes of this kind provide aid in setting up publishing firms, or short courses for publishing personnel. Such aid can also apply to printing technology and supplies. Old-fashioned printing machinery is heavy, durable, repairable, and still a highly effective technology. Donations of old printing machinery are a worthwhile form of aid, and in many cases more useful than the more impressive but infinitely more vulnerable electronic publishing technology. Help with the manufacture of paper and other materials such as inks is highly appropriate. The other book trades, too, are ripe for development. Until a local bookbinding cooperative was set up recently in Botswana, any binding had to be sent out of the country, and it was not unheard of for South African officials to stop consignments at the border on suspicion that they contained 'subversive' materials.

What is necessary then is aid that will enable Africa's knowledge base, and thus her library collections, to develop. No amount of book donations can achieve this, and in fact many of the donations that do arrive would be far better if they were pulped. This might at least provide some new paper, a basic resource which Africa needs more urgently than other countries' cast-off books. Africa's library collections are in such a dire state that a great deal of effort is needed to bring them up to a level which will meet the needs of current users, let alone attract a wider clientele. In research libraries the situation is so bad that the suggestion has been heard that help towards improving bibliographical access to Africana libraries outside the continent is the best way to supply Africa with access to its own documentary heritage. Even if, in the short term, this were true, it would represent a terrible admission of defeat and effectively close the door to future improvement. "Africa for the Africans" may have been the cry of the politicians at the time of independence, but as far as Africa's library collections are concerned it has a rather hollow ring.

Bibliographies, catalogues and computers

Even where a basically sound library collection does exist, it can rarely be exploited to anywhere near its full potential without great persistence and reliance on serendipity. Bibliographically, Africa is poorly served. National bibliographies exist in a good number of countries, but they are incomplete, biased towards books (particularly books in the metropolitan languages), and too out of date to be useful as acquisition tools. Subject bibliographies, abstracts and indexes are published mainly in the developed countries and are overwhelmingly directed towards formal literature from those parts of the world. Their use in acquisition exaggerates the tendency of libraries to lack the necessary African perspective and confirms their dependence on western publishing. In retrieving references for the user, librarians understandably gravitate towards the well-organized and seemingly comprehensive tools from the industrialized countries, in preference to the struggle they know they are likely to have in finding out about publications from their own or other African countries.

The influence of bibliographies from other parts of the world also has its effect on cataloguing in Africa. Cavan McCarthy, who worked for some time in Nigeria, argues that Africa's worship of the canon of Anglo-American cataloguing is yet another aspect of dependence. He paints a picture of librarians puzzling over tortuous and complex cataloguing rules to the extent where the backlog of umprocessed books waiting to be catalogued is more extensive than the actual library collection available on the open shelves. He describes the whole exercise of cataloguing according to the dictates of AACR/ISBD (Anglo American Cataloguing Rules/International Standard Book Description) as being a gross waste of human time and effort. He blames Western librarians originally for encouraging these cataloguing practices, and Third World librarians, by default, for letting them flourish. However, as he says, "cataloguers all over the world follow them, because they purport to be the best Western practice, because there are no decent alternatives, and because adoption leads to world bibliographical unity (on our terms)".[23]

This is taken to its extreme when African library systems acquire magnificent but immensely expensive tools such as the National Union Catalog (NUC) from the USA as a source for authoritative cataloguing practice. This not only contributes to over-elaborate and costly entries, but also leads to material that can be traced in the tool being given unjustified priority in the cataloguing process. Locally published material is frequently extremely difficult bibliographically, lacking essential details of imprint or appearing in languages the cataloguers cannot read, so it is not surprising if it is neglected in favour of imported material for which there is published cataloguing authority.

Catalogues in general are uneven and unreliable. Kenyan libraries, for instance, vary from a few which do not catalogue material at all, through a majority which catalogue monographs but not pamphlets or other less substantial items, to some research libraries which are able to produce analytical entries for their users.[24] The complexity of cataloguing practice contributes to this disparity at a very basic level. For instance, the thirty or so students each year on the Kenyan Library Assistants Certificate course are taught the Anglo-American Cataloguing Rules, second edition (AACR2), in all their intricate details. The expectation is that they will use these rules in their libraries, but as noted by McCarthy, the tendency is for cataloguing by AACR2 to be much too slow and inclined to produce backlogs. What is more, it can contribute to the production of unhelpful and mistake-ridden entries. The name under which an item is catalogued is the key to easy retrieval, yet conventional cataloguing codes show an inability to cope adequately with African personal names. With this in mind, the Kenya Library Association has produced a helpful set of guidelines on personal names, but ironically this important contribution to better cataloguing is not universally known or used in the country.

The dictates of classification systems, whether Dewey, Library of Congress, or Universal Decimal Classification, place material in what, for Africa, are unhelpful or downright misleading relationships. This can be blatantly racist at its worst. There was a chorus of distress from African librarians over the proposed changes in the recently revised twentieth edition of the Dewey Decimal Classification (DDC 20). On the advice of the South African Institute for Library and Information Services, this was to confirm the position of white South African history in the history part of the schedules, and black South African history amongst social problems. It also provided *de facto* recognition to South Africa's Bantustans. This episode shows that African librarians are developing a heartening awareness of the implications of the 'neutral' science of classification. Nevertheless, in hundreds of smaller, less glaring, ways, the most widely used classification systems continue to guarantee that, for the majority of users, Africa's library collections are organised in an alien and unhelpful way.

So far the continent's librarians have failed to seek remedies for these problems in more basic approaches to information retrieval, but are tending increasingly to look to information technology as a means of 'leapfrogging' whole development stages. As outlined in Chapter One, the positive image of technology is such that it is constantly forgotten that it can create more problems than it solves if it is used in an inappropriate context, or adopted for the wrong reasons. That the African context for library use of information technology is, for most types of library, inappropriate, is an argument that can be maintained very strongly. It is illuminating that, whilst government and commerce in Africa have in many cases made some worthwhile use of new technology, librarians are not much beyond the stage of talking about it. Since there is comparatively little experience of the actual working of automated library systems, or of the creation and use of on-line data bases, it is still possible for librarians to talk of them as if they were capable of providing marvellous improvements to service as if by magic.

The lack of local suppliers, maintenance engineers, and a consistent electrical supply, not to mention the very slight prospect of the indigenous development of hardware or software industries in the near future, are very serious limitations on the effective use of computer technology even for merely in-house purposes. This applies whether mainframes or personal computers are being considered. Governments which are making real improvements to such basic services as their electricity supply industries are probably making as big a contribution to the future prospects for information technology as those which have actually installed large quantities of computer hardware.

Making good decisions on the purchase of systems is notoriously difficult, and gifts of computers have tended to be as mixed a blessing to libraries as gifts of books. Some donor governments have given either what they want to get rid of or what will benefit their own high-tech industries. Whether these machines are suitable for library purposes hardly seems to be a consideration. The University of Botswana Library, for instance, found that the machine provided for it had virtually never had library applications software written for it. Only two sets of software that offered some possibility of being usable in the library's circumstances could be discovered worldwide, one from Australia and the other from South Africa. This narrowing of choice did not offer good prospects for the successful implementation of an automated system. This type of difficulty, and the potential of incautiously applied or inefficiently maintained technology for causing almost unimaginable chaos within an organization seldom features in the debate.

In an elegant and provocative address to the fifty-third IFLA Conference at Brighton, U.K. in 1987, K.M. Aithnard, Director General of the publishing house, Nouvelles Editions Africaines, in Togo, expressed his bewilderment whenever he came across the terms 'library' and 'developing country' in the same sentence. He proceeded to outline how libraries convey certain values according to their contents, and are a concrete expression of the achievements and aspirations of the particular societies in which they have developed. He therefore found it difficult to comprehend ''the fact that people think it is essential to set up structures and infrastructures, deriving from a centuries old tradition, in other countries where the context is quite different. In other words, things are always presented as if all the changes necessary in the materially poor countries should not only be modelled on the well-off countries but should also repeat a supposedly linear process having the same objectives".[25] Many others who have written about libraries in Africa have not failed to notice the anomalies this produces, but unfortunately the library model which has been 'parachuted' into Africa, marked as it is by self-doubt and contradictions even at source, is sufficiently institutionalized to make change seem impossibly difficult. Yet change there must be if library and information work on the African continent is not to wither quietly away and die.

Librarians and dependence

As yet, solutions to Africa's library crisis have failed to materialize, and at best can only be discerned as a faint glimmer on a distant horizon. A great deal of effort, as well as creative thinking, will have to be involved in order to change or replace existing systems and modes of thought, which have had twenty to thirty years to ossify. It is to Africa's library profession that we must turn for this, and it is the character of that profession that will determine what radical solutions, if any, will be proposed and which changes will be accepted.

The record of Africa's library profession in responding to change has been generally disappointing. It has rarely managed to implement new ideas, and as a result has remained firmly tied to a colonial past which has little to offer to an Africa in transition. This almost total dependence on the past can be witnessed in the profession's preoccupation with status, in the patterns of staffing it has cultivated, and more obviously in the design of library education programmes that have been adopted.

The amount of documentation that has been produced on library education in Africa is quite disproportionate to what actually exists in terms of programmes and what has been achieved in terms of the quality of those programmes. If the amount of energy, effort and time that has been expended in writing about library education in Africa had been devoted to developing and improving actual programmes, then by now Africa might have the best-educated librarians in the whole world. The focus of our attention here will therefore be on how the structure and training of Africa's library and information workforce has contributed to Africa's library dependence and the struggle in which the continent's libraries are now embroiled.

Leaders or workers

The main impetus for the development of public libraries in Africa can be traced back to Unesco's Ibadan Seminar which took place in 1953.[26] This meeting not only championed the creation of public libraries as part of an integrated national development plan, but also provided the framework that would define the structure and character of the library profession as a whole. It also laid the foundations for the education and training of Africa's library personnel. The doubtful legacy of the Ibadan Seminar still survives today, and has subsequently spread beyond the narrow concerns of public librarianship to infect the entire body of Africa's library profession. It is clearly discernible in the anxiety and tension that surrounds any discussion of staffing structures and standards, employment needs and programmes for education and training. It is not unfair to say that it represents the single most important factor inhibiting the change that is necessary if librarianship in Africa is to survive.[27]

The Seminar advocated the creation of a leadership cadre that would be able to provide a suitably elevated professional profile. This in turn, it was felt, would result in a more ready acceptance of the continent's emerging library movement. There was, however, another approach, advocated by some participants, that placed much more stress on training workers who would perform the everyday tasks of librarianship. There has been debate on this ever since. In Nigeria during the 1970s it became particularly heated when Ahmadu Bello University launched an undergraduate degree in library studies. This raised a storm of protest from Ibadan University which until then had dictated the character of the profession's leaders through its postgraduate programmes.

The Ibadan Seminar recommendations confirmed the already-emerging stratification of Africa's library workforce into very precisely defined layers of leaders (professionals) and workers (non- or para-professionals). The status of the expatriates who established services throughout most of newly-independent Africa confirmed this division. Categorization of staff was, naturally enough, a normal feature of the library systems from which they came, but sharper definition of such divisions was essential to the structure of colonial societies. In colonial or immediately post-colonial Africa the categorization of library personnel took the form: 'professional = expatriate' and 'non-professional = African'. Once established with such sharp distinction, the division gradually assumed the force of a natural law. After the expatriates had gone, African professionals took on not only the professional tasks and responsibilities, but the very rigid definitions of the difference between professional and non-professional staff which came with them. The way in which this developed subsequently shows why it was not a happy legacy.

The legacy is unquestionably alive, and is evidenced in the position of that section of the library and information workforce that is categorized as para-professional. This type of worker is sufficiently trained to perform many professional tasks, but the system will not permit them the means to obtain professional responsibility. This unfortunate position, although rooted in colonial tradition, was also a response to the shortage of fully professional personnel immediately after independence. Three decades on since independence para-professionals are a permanent and distinct stratum of employee on much the same terms as they were then. Although they have acquired considerable skills and knowledge at Africa's own library schools, staffing structures offer them only routine clerical tasks. Their position varies slightly from country to country, but they have usually taken a diploma in library studies which can be of two or three years' duration. There is also a less fortunate category, who have only a certificate in library studies obtained after a course of six or sometimes even eighteen months of study.[28] Transition from certificate to diploma is usually possible after further study, but diploma holders are, in the majority of cases, barred from advancement to the professional ranks. Their status and previous educational background do not qualify them for the graduate study which is now the accepted norm for entry into the professional ranks.

To make the situation even more complex, an idea which received some attention in Asia a few years ago is now receiving some interest in Africa. This is the idea of the 'barefoot librarian', which threatens to add yet another category of non-professional staff to library establishments.[29] Several types of public service in developing countries are responding to the influence of the so-called 'barefoot revolution', and it is no surprise that this should have been taken up by librarians. The idea is basically that workers are recruited from the community, trained at a very elementary level in the techniques needed to perform the required work, whatever it be, are employed, usually on a part-time basis, for a small salary or honorarium. In the history of library practice a good number of examples of this approach can be found, although not described by this term. In Tanzania, for instance, rural reading room attendants are employed on this basis, and it seems possible that the principle will be adopted elsewhere. It is, first of all, a reaction to the expense of services that are based on current practice in industrialized countries. Secondly, interest in it arises from the perception that established services with their associated forms of staffing have failed to adjust to local needs and circumstances.

The danger which comes from the barefoot librarian is not in the essential concept of a category of worker, qualified more by their base in the community than by the level of their academic achievement, and providing an unpretentious and appropriate service to that same community. Rather it is that library systems will use the idea merely as a way of nominally expanding their services on the cheap. Unless the need to give effective training to these barefoot librarians, and provide them with constant support and encouragement, is fully recognized, then the system will produce yet another disaffected and inefficient level of employee. The information requirements of rural communities will be poorly served if this happens. Those barefoot librarians who do manage to make some success of their work will also certainly develop legitimate ambitions for more regular and better paid employment within the library service. Library employers must anticipate this and provide the channels for advancement that will meet these ambitions. Africa's library services to date have not had an encouraging record in developing such opportunities in their staffing structures, and while one would like to be optimistic about the barefoot concept, the probability is that it will only succeed in creating another even less well-qualified 'non-professional' category of employee.

Although the structure of library employment had from the first been defined in terms of 'them and us', the implications of local professional control of systems (that the 'us' part of the system would one day be African too) was recognized. This had to be achieved through the education and training of an African professional workforce. The form that professional training took was usually dependent on what types of training were available in the colonial or former colonial country. Correspondence courses for the Associateship of the (British) Library Association, then full-time courses in Britain for the same qualification, were an early response. Since the Associateship and the Fellowship (which could be obtained by the same methods), were qualifications which the expatriates themselves possessed, it was perhaps predictable that their African replacements should also wish to obtain them too.

The move towards degree level entry to the library profession in the

United Kingdom during the 1960s and 1970s had a disastrous effect. The African elite of Associates and Fellows of the Library Association, who had been among the first librarians in Anglophone Africa to achieve professional status, suddenly seemed to be transformed from professionals and demoted, in the eyes of many, to the ranks of the para-professionals. Many of them returned overseas, having little choice but to enrol in various British and American library education programmes, in order for their professionalism to be confirmed anew. They studied alongside a new generation of graduate African librarians who were receiving their first professional training overseas, providing ample opportunity for schisms to occur in the professional ranks. The outcome was that some professional librarians were now deemed more professional than others.

These overseas programmes, which over the years have served the needs of the majority of African professional librarians, have been repeatedly criticized as being too remote from the geographical, cultural, social, economic and political realities of library work in Africa.[30] It is the standard currency of debate on library education in Africa to cite instances of members of staff who have been sent to prestigious library schools in Europe and America and returned with a great deal of irrelevant knowledge and a grossly inflated idea of their ability to perform the duties of senior posts in their institutions. Aside from the fact that many of those who proffer these arguments themselves went through this same educational process, much of what they say is perfectly valid. Specifically, overseas postgraduate programmes have been criticized as being too short and intensive, concentrating on theory and broad issues to the virtual exclusion of practice. Further criticism centres around programmes concerning themselves exclusively with issues of concern to the industrial countries, with only minor compensation being offered through the availability of options on comparative and international librarianship. Although these are often taught by lecturers who have a good deal of experience in developing countries, they are not always supported by sufficient information resources on libraries in development.

Despite such criticism, common to many professional fields, the popularity of overseas programmes has never slackened, even when appropriate local alternatives are available. It is not surprising, therefore, that the present generation of leaders in African librarianship contains many who pay generous tribute to the opportunity that was provided for them to study overseas. The worthwhile experiences gained by the individual can be appreciated by reading that excellent, and rare, autobiography of a librarian, Stanley Made's *Made in Zimbabwe*. He had the exhilarating sense that he was "breaking new ground for sowing the seeds of a new or a hitherto not very well known profession by my fellow Africans".[31] The fact is that these programmes were originally designed for their home countries, and make very good sense in terms of their own needs. They are in many ways not directly relevant to Africa's needs and require that the African student applies a great deal of critical faculty to their content. Despite the ability of many students to do this, the programmes have not always helped African librarians in sorting out their views on priorities for the library systems of their own countries.

Partly in response to these criticisms, Africa started to develop library education programmes of its own. This initially led to the establishment of the Institute of Librarianship at Ibadan University, shortly followed by the Library School in Accra, which subsequently became part of the University of Ghana, Legon. The next stage was the foundation of regional library schools, firstly in Dakar, Senegal, for librarians, archivists, and documentalists from Francophone Africa, which is still flourishing today. This was followed by the East African School of Librarianship at Makerere University, Uganda, originally designed to cater for all the Eastern African countries, but now sadly in decline. More than thirty years after the Ibadan Seminar, many of the countries of the continent can boast a library school or some type of training programme, and plans exist for quite a few more.

Most African library schools began with certificate and diploma programmes for para-professionals, and in some cases this is still all that is offered. There is no precise international standard for the distinction between certificates and diplomas, nor for that matter any real precedent to guide the curriculum planner who is required to draw up two separate curricula preserving a clear distinction between two categories of para-professional librarianship. Generally speaking the certificate is reserved for entrants at a lower level of educational qualification, and may, in some cases, lead on to admission to the diploma. Only the fact that the entrant's educational qualifications are usually below university entrance requirements, and that the programmes offer very little general educational content beyond librarianship, seriously distinguishes them from degree and even postgraduate programmes in librarianship.

To the outsider, the system no doubt looks over-elaborate. The existence of two levels of para-professional qualification certainly overstates the quantity of knowledge needed for someone to work in a library. Those who do manage to break out of the straitjacket of non-professionalism and progress onwards through diploma and degree to postgraduate level, certainly find that there is a great deal of overlap and repetition between the various levels. The certificate has little to offer as the path to a career, and the diploma in turn takes holders only as far as the barrier which separates them from the professional posts. Since the diploma undoubtedly prepares them for much of the content of professional work, the para-professional staff working in Africa's libraries feel an understandable distress and frustration at their inability to progress further.[32]

Despite years of talk there seems to be virtually no progress in devising a means by which para-professionals can jump the gap to achieve professional status. Indeed, in Botswana, the ladder of education and promotion that enabled one former Director of the Botswana National Library Service to rise to the top from one of the lowest grades is no longer really effective. Even where programmes do exist that in theory make it possible for diploma holders to apply for an undergraduate degree, they often find themselves competing for admission against school leavers with better academic credentials, who are often admitted first. Until there is a recognition of the amount and quality of study involved in obtaining these diplomas, librarianship in Africa is condemned to have many of its practitioners in a state of disaffection so serious as to inhibit their will to contribute.

This disaffection is only made worse by the staffing situation at professional level. Despite the rigid hierarchy between professional and non-professional personnel, there is no similar stratification in the tasks each category performs. This has been noted, not only by casual observation, but also through survey[33] and has been graphically highlighted by C.C. Aguolu, a researcher who attempted to ascertain levels of job satisfaction in Nigeria's university libraries:

> In one university, one librarian with an honours degree in physics was doing no book selection, no reference work, and no subject cataloguing of scientific and technical publications. He was primarily filing cards, keeping records of gifts and exchanges and occasionally participating in order work. This librarian put his disappointment in this way: "I think I am wasting my time here." There were similar cases in other library departments. In another university, three librarians with degrees in the biological and physical sciences were confined to the cataloguing department, never involved in any scientific and technical bibliographical work, reference and information service, let alone in book selection.[34]

It is not surprising, therefore, to find that library education at professional level is not free from the type of problem previously associated with the training of para-professionals. Whilst in Britain a bachelor's degree in librarianship is considered a fully adequate qualification for professional status, this is not the case in North America, where a master's degree is the bare minimum for most types of post. African library systems tend towards the American version, which means that even if the para-professionals could be helped to achieve bachelor's degrees in library studies, the system would ensure that their professional contribution would yet again be severely restricted. What is more, a postgraduate qualification is often taken to mean not just the postgraduate diploma, which up until recently was very much the most usual qualification at this level in Britain, but a full master's degree. This is certainly the case for many posts in Africa with academic status, and to pile on the weight even further, a doctoral degree is often required for elevation to the most senior positions. As most institutions of library education in Africa feel themselves unready to offer such qualifications, this takes many of Africa's most able library personnel overseas for long periods, at a time when their energy and motivation are at their highest levels and when their services are urgently needed back home.

The rigidity of attitudes towards staffing structures has turned the attention of Africa's library educators too much towards levels of library qualifications, while diverting them away from pressing questions of curriculum content. The content of Africa's library education programmes reflects the fundamental difficulties arising from the conjunction of a library ethos drawn from a Western print-based culture and the needs of developing but information-poor societies. The fact is that Africa's library education programmes are little better in terms of relevance to Africa's needs than those of the metropolitan countries. This is not to say that African library educators have been impervious to the need for curricula to be more responsive to African circumstances, just that the results of their concern are not entirely convincing. During a recent regional seminar on library education in Africa, this was boldly argued by Kingo Mchombu who said that:

> the call for relevance over the last twenty years or so had simply led us to dress up conventional subjects in an 'African shirt'. What we often end up talking about is librarianship in Africa, not African librarianship. Library schools have only succeeded in producing librarians who are capable of serving an elite—we have failed to produce people appropriate to our real needs.[35]

The familiarity of the content of curricula in African library schools can be substantiated from the briefest of glances through their calendars, brochures and prospectuses. Even at diploma level, library management seems to be taught in the usual terms of organizational structures and may include elements on a rich variety of budgeting techniques. This despite the fact that most library systems are comparatively small, have few staff, and often very limited funds to budget for. There is a predictably thorough treatment of cataloguing, classification, and indexing, while bibliography, including historical bibliography, still looms large. Options on such topics as bibliometrics, advanced information retrieval and music librarianship, are often offered as if they were central to the work of both professional and non-professional.

The case for developing a curriculum with a strong emphasis on content that will have relevance to the mass of the population is a compelling one. The needs are so great and the resources for meeting them so limited that library school curricula drawn up on idealized lines cannot be considered adequate. At a time when Africa's library educators were starting to take steps in the right direction, the issue has been confused as a result of the activities of a number of international organizations. They are promoting a different set of prescriptions for library and information education programmes in Africa. These include the teaching of information science and such approaches as the harmonization of curricula across the entire spectrum of the information professions.

The plan by Unesco and the International Development Research Centre (IDRC) to create a regional postgraduate information science programme for Africa is worth highlighting in this connection. These organizations published a report in 1985 which described the process by which an appropriate location for the programme had been selected.[36] Two possible locations, Ibadan University, Nigeria, and Addis Ababa University, Ethiopia, were identified, the former to cater to the needs of West Africa, and the latter to develop a constituency in Southern, Central, and Eastern Africa. The mission report presents virtually no qualitative information as a basis for these decisions. There is little argument in justification of the programme, except familiar comments on the importance of information and development, and no quantitative analysis of the existing need for such a programme beyond a vague assurance that there would be a considerable market. One of the few stated reasons for the choice of Addis Ababa as a location was the congenial international milieu of

African dignitaries, embassy officials, United Nations representatives and employees of the world's aid agencies. Anthony Olden points out that, in contrast, "no mention is made of the famine in the country-side or the $119 per capita income".[37]

Olden did not comment on the next stage, for after Addis Ababa was selected, the curriculum was apparently designed by a task force on the basis of a world trip visiting institutions of information science education on a lengthy itinerary including South and North America and Europe. The objectives of these trips were clearly identified by Unesco and IDRC as being to "acquaint members of the task force with the main aspects of the functioning of these institutions and to identify the issues and problems that the University of Addis Ababa might have to face in establishing its own information science programme".[38] Despite all this, the whole exercise has been an expensive failure, for between 1983, when the original choice of Addis Ababa was made, and 1989, not a single student has graduated from the programme.

As will be evident from the arguments offered in Chapter Two, there is a pressing need for solutions to Africa's information crisis. So far, answers have not been forthcoming from Africa's library professionals, and the idea of training a new class of information professionals with an information science background incorporating systems analysis, research methods, data base management, and policy design is certainly attractive. The development of programmes which will largely cater for a narrow band of the population who are already information-rich, is not necessarily incompatible with a more egalitarian approach to curriculum design which attempts to develop an information workforce for service to the majority who are information-poor. The two approaches are, however, distinct from each other and it is essential to ensure that the one approach, equipped as it is with the attractions of technology, and a fashionable image, does not overpower the other. Just as with library education, the roots of information science education must be firmly set in Africa and there are, as yet, few signs that this is fully appreciated. The danger that information science education will be an immensely costly irrelevance, worse than the failures of library education, is a very immediate one.

Conclusion

Africa's libraries and other information institutions urgently need to break the dependence on Western values which continues to retard their development. Dependence is not invariably harmful— witness the benefits that some smaller European nations have gained from their close and dependent ties with the German economy—but its economic effects on Africa have been consistently damaging. In terms of library and information work in Africa, we would argue that the same is true. If this is indeed the case, the question arises as to whether the necessary distancing can be achieved. Dependence is as much a psychological phenomenon as an economic one. Indeed, economic chains do not always bind as strongly as those of the mind. To break away from an unwanted dependence is, therefore, not at all easy. What is more, in this case it may, in the short-term, increase the poverty that afflicts African information institutions.

To be poor is bad, but to be locked into relationships that limit the options for breaking out of that poverty is worse. These relationships can be changed. It is essential for Africa's library and information community to struggle to avoid dependence on international publishing and bookselling companies, to ensure that donor agencies do not set the parameters of what can be done by the nature of the assistance they give, or that telecommunication and computer technology do not create patterns of information flow incompatible with developing country aims. Even more important than this, however, is the need to combat the psychological dependence which is nurtured by modes of thought and philosophies developed in other parts of the world, where both information needs and the resources to meet them are quite different. The imported attitudes and preconceptions of librarianship which dominate in Africa at present both permit and encourage the ways in which this dependency manifests itself. Inappropriate decisions over such matters as the planning of library buildings, the purchase of materials, or the grading and training of staff, are made not just because advice or commercial pressures from outside suggest them, but because in the minds of those making the decisions there is already the propensity to make them. It is in the minds of the information professionals that we will find the roots of dependence and this is where the changes need to occur that will permit the development of a genuinely African librarianship.

The institution in which this must take place first of all is the one where ideas on library and information work are formed, namely, the library school. Change in library education is therefore central to eliminating the dependence syndrome and providing the impetus to direct future generations of information workers towards new service priorities more in tune with Africa's real needs. Whether this is a realizable objective or not should become clearer in the remaining chapters when we will examine more closely what Africa's librarians themselves have said about their predicament, and what actions they have intitiated to forge a more African library identity.

References

1. Kotei, S.I.A. Some cultural and social factors of book reading and publishing in Africa. *In*: Oluwasanmi, E. *and others eds. Publishing in Africa in the Seventies.* Ife, Nigeria, University of Ife Press, 1975. 174–208.
2. Goody, J. Introduction. *In*: Goody, J. *ed. Literacy in Traditional Society.* New York, Cambridge University Press, 1968. 1–26.
3. Flood, R.A. *Public libraries in the colonies.* London, Library Association, 1951. (Library Association Pamphlet no. 5). p 33.
4. Wilks, I. The transmission of Islamic learning in the Western Sudan. *In*: Goody, J. *ed, op. cit.* 161–197.
5. Maack, M.N. The colonial legacy in West African libraries: a comparative study. *In*: *Advances in Librarianship*, 12, 1982. 173–245.
6. Aguolu, C.C. Father of Nigerian librarianship. *New Library World*, 79, 1978. 251–253.
7. Benge, R.C. *Cultural crisis and libraries in the third world*, London, Bingley, 1979.
8. Broome, M. First steps in Tanganyika. *East Africa Library Association Bulletin*, 7, 1966. 18–25.
9. Harris, M. The purpose of the American public library: a Revisionist interpretation of history. *In*: Totterdell, B. *ed. Public library purpose: a reader.* London, Bingley, 1978. p 49.
10. Kigongo-Bukenya, C. The Public Libraries Board in Uganda. *In*: Wallenius, A.B. *ed. Libraries in East Africa.* Uppsala, Scandinavian Institute of African Studies, 1971. 145–162.
11. Parker, J.S. *Unesco and library development planning.* London, Library Association, 1985.
12. Brewster, B. *American overseas library technical assistance, 1940–1970.* Metuchen, N.J., Scarecrow Press, 1976.
13. Gunton, D. *Books, libraries and aid, in particular British aid in Nigeria during the development decade 1960–1969.* Unpublished M.A. Thesis, University of Sheffield, 1974.
14. Coombs, D. *Spreading the word: the library work of the British Council.* London, Mansell, 1988.
15. Olden, A. *The beneficiaries of library and information policy in British and ex-British Africa.* (Ph.D. dissertation) University of Illinois at Urbana-Champaign, 1987.
16. Plumbe, W.J. Climate as a factor in the planning of University Library Buildings. *Unesco Bulletin for libraries*, 17, 1963. 316–325.
17. Kotei, S.I.A. Some variables and comparison between developed and developing library systems. *International Library Review*, 9, 1977. 249–267.
18. Jones, K.H. Towards a re-interpretation of public library purpose. *In*:

Totterdell, B. *ed. Public library purpose: a reader.* London, Bingley, 1978. 123-124.

19. Maack, M. The role of external aid in West African library development. *Library Quarterly*, 56, 1986. 1-16.

20. Harris, J. Ibadan University Library: some notes on its birth and growth. *Library Association Record*, 67, 1965. 256-257.

21. Membury, D. The Ranfurly Library Service and the Textbooks for Africa Project. *African Research and Documentation*, 46, 1988. 40-46.

22. Kirkwood, K. [Letter]. *The Times,* January 2nd, 1988.

23. McCarthy, C. Colonial cataloguing. *New Library World*, 76, 1975. 55.

24. Thairu, R.W. Cataloguing policies and problems in Kenyan Libraries. *African Research and Documentation*, 40, 1986. 8-15.

25. Aithnard, K.M. *Is the library a source of information in the developing countries.* Paper presented at IFLA General Conference, Brighton, U.K., August, 1987.

26. Unesco. *Development of public libraries in Africa: the Ibadan Seminar.* Paris, Unesco, 1954. (Public library manuals, no. 6).

27. Gibbons, F. *and* Neill, J.R. *eds* Education and training for librarianship and information work in Southern, Central, and Eastern Africa. *In:* Asamani, J.O. *and others eds. Libraries and Literacy. Proceedings of the Seventh Meeting of the Standing Conference of Eastern, Central and Southern African Librarians, Gaborone, 4-8 Aug, 1986.* Gaborone, Botswana Library Association, 1987. 180-202.

28. Bock, G. *and* Huttemann, L. *eds. Curriculum adjustments in information studies training programmes in Africa.* Bonn, DSE, 1987.

29. Wijasuriya, D., Lim H-T. *and* Nadarajah, R. *The barefoot librarian: library development in South East Asia with special reference to Malaysia.* London, Bingley, 1975.

30. Lundu, M.C. Library education and training: at home or abroad? *International Library Review*, 14, 1982. 363-378.

31. Made, S. *Made in Zimbabwe.* Gweru, Mambo Press, 1980.

32. Sturges, P. What librarians feel about their careers: a survey of diploma and certificate holders. *Botswana Library Association Journal*, 7, 1985. 9-21.

33. Neill, J.R. Library manpower planning in Southern, Central and Eastern Africa. *In:* Huttemann, L. *ed. Manpower training needs. Proceedings and papers of the information experts meeting, Harare, Zimbabwe, 1985.* Bonn, DSE, 1985. 19-28.

34. Aguolu, C.C. Staffing in Nigerian university libraries. *Library Review*, 31, 1982. p 21.

35. Mchombu, K.J. [Statement in discussion]. *In:* Gibbons, F. *and* Neill, J.R. *op. cit.* p 198.

36. Roberts, K.H. *ed. Regional postgraduate program in information science in Anglophone Africa: identification of an appropriate location. Report of a joint Unesco/IDRC mission.* Ottawa, IDRC, 1986.

37. Olden, A. Sub-Saharan Africa and the paperless society. *Journal of the American Society for Information Science*, 38, 1987. p 302.

Chapter Four

The Search for Relevance

Introduction

During the late 1960s and early 1970s, after the excitement of the early years of independence when new systems were begun and the possibilities seemed infinite, a mood of perplexity and frustration overcame Africa's library profession. Governments became disenchanted with libraries' lack of tangible achievement, and librarians failed to plead an effective case for the help that might have enabled them to produce better results. As the situation deteriorated, the tendency to evade the real issues increased. It was at this same time, however, that the voices of African librarians started to be heard more frequently at international conferences, and appeared in written form in professional journals and academic theses. At first, much of what they said provided only limited insight into the actual condition of Africa's libraries. Resolutions and plans were described as if they were a functioning reality, and the day-to-day consequences of the problems influencing library development in the continent were not much discussed. Many of the growing archives of consultancy reports and expert missions on library development also tended to skirt round the harsher realities and discuss services as if they could exist in a vacuum. There was a tendency to understate the extent of structural problems and the influence of external circumstances.

The library profession had identified the issue of libraries and national development as being of the first importance. This was potentially a very fruitful approach to the tasks of justifying and designing services, and it provided a full agenda for discussion from the mid-1970s through to the late 1980s. However, what was said progressed little further than repeated assertions that libraries could perform a vital role in development. Defining that role in a way that convinced the decision makers and made real differences to the services provided seems seldom to have been achieved. Despite this, the formula still maintains on the African profession's psyche a grip which seems likely to endure well into the next decade. The adoption of national development as the key issue seems fairly clearly to have arisen from the spread of awareness amongst library and information professionals of Unesco's NATIS (National Information Systems) concept. This aimed to bring a broad, integrated perspective to the planning of a country's library and information sector.

NATIS and the programmes associated with it, such as UNISIST (Unesco/International Council of Scientific Unions programme for the development of a world science information system), UBC (Universal Bibliographical Control), PGI (General Information Programme), UAP (Universal Availability of Publications) and RAMP (Records and Archives Management Programme), have propagated a considerable mass of literature in the form of journal articles, dissertations, theses, and reports. They have also enabled an extensive international dialogue to take place through visiting consultancies and international conferences. Some countries can show institutions whose very existence they owe to these programmes, such as national bibliographic centres set up as pilot projects with money provided as part of the UBC programme. Archives and records work seems quite frequently to have gained some real advantages from RAMP projects. Yet despite this it is not unfair to consider NATIS, and some of the other programmes, as having failed to produce results commensurate with the attention that the information professions have paid to them.

The belief that libraries and other information institutions have a vital and irreplaceable role in national planning and national development is both implicit and explicit in much that has been published by organizations such as Unesco, IFLA, and the German Foundation for International Development (DSE). They have certainly acted with goodwill and in full confidence that what they have encouraged African librarians to believe is both true and to their professional advantage. Whilst we would not deny that this idea has an essential core of truth, we feel that its use in constructing arguments in favour of particular schemes and projects has not been of real professional advantage. It is too strong a formulation of the utility of library and information services, and it just cannot be proved in a way that is sufficiently conclusive to make it helpful in dealing with governments and their agencies which fund such services. Many theses on the theme of libraries and national development, and some of the published articles and reports, have employed unconvincing methodology and drawn tenuous inferences from a meagre base of information to support their attempts to achieve this proof.

Encouragingly, throughout the 1980s a growing number of African librarians have started to adopt rather different approaches. They have discussed systems and services with a degree of openness and candour which, in the past, was not always present. This has often called for some courage. As Shiraz Durrani puts it, "Over the years, the younger generation of librarians have questioned the basis of library services but their views and creativity have been suppressed as being 'non-professional'."[1] Despite the resistance of those whose position in the hierarchy leads them to cling to the status quo, new views are emerging, and becoming sufficiently accepted to constitute the nucleus of a movement. It has been conveniently labelled 'African librarianship', and although not yet properly conceptualized, articulated or set down on paper, does provide the first glimmerings of hope for the future for the library in Africa. We will examine the content of this search for a more relevant African librarianship, through both of these phases, in this chapter.

Integrated library planning and national development

The predominant themes for Africa's libraries from the mid-1970s onwards have, as we have suggested, originated in the series of Unesco programmes, NATIS, UNISIST, and PGI. Unesco's NATIS and UNISIST programmes, which were later integrated in the General Information Programme (PGI) were broadly-conceived strategies intended to encourage countries to adopt a more systematic approach to planning for information provision. NATIS was intended to stimulate the creation of comprehensive national networks for information of all kinds, so as to eliminate duplication, make resources available more widely, and provide the user with the information required in a swift and effective way. UNISIST was essentially concerned with fostering the organization of scientific and technical information in individual countries so they each could contribute to, and draw upon, a world-wide pool of information, through the international exchange of materials.

In 1976 an overall programme designed to accommodate both

NATIS and UNISIST was adopted by Unesco, and provided with the acronym PGI, derived from the French wording of its title, which in English is General Information Programme. The five main themes of PGI were summed up as:

1. Promotion of information policies and plans (both at national and other levels);
2. Promotion of methods, norms and standards for dealing with information;
3. Contributing to the development of information infrastructures;
4. Contributing to the development of specialized information systems;
5. Promotion of the education and training of information specialists and users.

As summarized by Jacques Tocatlian and Aziz Abid, "PGI promotes the creation of libraries, archives, and information services as well as that of units responsible for referral, analysis, consolidation and repackaging of information, data compilation, and information on on-going research and other functions contributing to the flow of information from the source to the user."[2] Stated thus, PGI seems the essence of simplicity, whereas the history of the programme, and of the predecessors which now form part of it, has had more of the character of a well-meant but unworkable complex of ideas.

The sheer volume of words in the form of guidelines, studies, country reports, consultancies, recommendations, proceedings of meetings, conferences, workshops, seminars, training courses, colloquia, and so on, is in some ways impressive, but has also created considerable confusion. No one single message, that could have been easily presented to government ministers and officials as the advice of the world library and information community, has yet emerged from all this effort. In summary, the types of criticism of Unesco's programmes that can be heard when informal discussion takes place at meetings of African librarians include: too little follow-through of missions to individual countries, inappropriate choice of institutions to act as 'focal points', too strong an emphasis on scientific materials and technological solutions, and a lack of help in discriminating between choices of alternative strategies which might be available. There is also a line of criticism of Unesco's programmes, sometimes voiced on such occasions, which suggests that, despite the stated intentions of the programmes, they have the tendency to increase the information dependency of developing countries on the information-rich countries of the North.

The story has been well told by the library and information consultant Stephen Parker, who not only chronicles the history of each individual programme, but also outlines Africa's contribution to their creation and development.[3] NATIS itself was largely under the shadow of the rival programme, UNISIST. This seems almost entirely to have been a matter of the internal politics of Unesco, rather than because of any major difficulty with the concept of NATIS. The outrage of Herman Liebars, then President of IFLA, at the coup that enabled the UNISIST programme to gain ascendancy over NATIS, is plain in the following statement which described it as:

> a brilliant example of successful international manoeuvring. A couple of clever people at the International Council of Scientific Unions' Abstracting Board realised that the scientific information division of Unesco had a very weak programme and proposed to them to reinvent the wheel.[4]

The reader who wishes to read a blow by blow account of the ensuing battle between these two rival programmes will have to turn to Parker's book. The only comment we would offer is that Africa's library professionals spent well over a decade in debating, discussing, and writing about these programmes, when their energy and efforts would have been better expended in continuing to grapple with the multitude of everyday problems that beset their services.

The main reason why this story is so sad is that there are virtually no practical results to be shown from Africa's involvement with these programmes. After almost twenty years they have contributed almost nothing to the development of Africa's information environment. Perhaps even sadder is the fact that this particular story appears to have no ending. By now there can hardly be a single country in Africa, however small and however lacking in libraries it may be, that has not had a NATIS-inspired model applied to it. The Seychelles is a good example. As early as 1977, a consultant prepared a plan for a national information system, despite the fact that the Seychelles at that time did not have a single qualified librarian. What is more, the findings of this consultancy could be added to what had been said by four other consultants who had previously visited these islands with a similar brief.[5] This example is not an isolated one, and the story of NATIS and related programmes shows how the attention of Africa's librarians has been diverted from the most crucial issues towards attractive but ultimately futile recipes for success.

Africa and NATIS

Africa's first real involvement with the NATIS concept took place in 1970, four years before the NATIS programme was formally called into existence at the 1974 Intergovernmental Conference. A meeting was convened by Unesco in Kampala, Uganda, which was to consider a document to be prepared by Charles Deane Kent, who was at the time Director of the Public Library and Art Museum in London, Ontario. Apart from the final report published by Unesco,[6] the documentation about this meeting is extremely slender, and only Parker gives some clue as to what actually went on, and more importantly what went wrong.[7] The plan for the meeting was that Kent would prepare a draft library development plan for Uganda which would be not merely the working document for the meeting, but eventually a model for the rest of the continent. Kent arrived on the scene to prepare his model plan just as Mr A.A. Nekyon was concluding a formal Inquiry into Uganda's Public Libraries Board. The report accused the Board, and a number of senior staff members, of inefficiency, incompetence, nepotism, mismanagement and malfeasance, which had brought the library service to virtual ruin. It was in this climate that Kent proceeded with his task. It is little wonder that the result was not the planning model for Uganda, or the rest of the continent, that Unesco had originally envisaged.

Nevertheless, the Kampala Meeting, which included a number of Africa's leading librarians, proceeded to prepare a set of guidelines for library development planning in Africa. The main focus of the recommendations centred around each country forming a single body that would be charged with the responsibility of developing an integrated library and information system that would be fully representative of all the nation's interests. This would be established under the aegis of a government ministry, and would play a decisive role in national development. The essentials of the NATIS approach are contained in this, with all their emphasis on structures within which library and information systems are supposed to grow and flourish. In hindsight, the emphasis seems like the reverse of what was really needed. Flexible response to specific needs so as to build strong individual services, such as libraries in government departments, series of publications for distribution to literacy centres, information officers answering queries in the headquarters of agricultural extension services, was where effort was needed. Structures to ensure balanced and well planned growth were much less important than the vitality of the separate initiatives that one day, if they were successful, might create the need for structures. Africa's contemporary view of the proceedings is barely documented except for a brief and wholly uncritical account by Ezekiel Kaungamno, Director of the Tanzania National Library Service. This account suggests that the meeting was of extreme importance and great relevance but fails to tell us just why that might be the case.[8]

As Parker points out, for Uganda the postscript to the Kampala Meeting occurred barely two months after the delegates had departed when:

> the Uganda Army seized control of the country in the absence of the President, Milton Obote, and on the following day Major General Idi Amin, Commander of the Army, proclaimed himself Head of State. There is little evidence to suggest that library development received much official attention during the Amin regime, and with the benefit of hindsight we can see now that, in the light of events in Uganda both before and after the Kampala Meeting, the selection of that country as a venue, at that moment in its history, was particularly unfortunate.[9]

The Kampala story is symbolic of the reasons why NATIS and similar programmes have had much less effect on African library and information circumstances than was hoped. In these very beginnings the creators of the programme took insufficient cognisance of Africa's library and information environment, and proceeded as if political and social conditions were an irrelevance. It is our contention that the idea of a single, national, integrated library and information system as the answer for Africa's library problems emerged from precisely this neglect of messy reality. Although its appropriateness was doubtful from the outset, and indeed, perhaps in a perverse way just because it was concerned with issues one step removed from the struggle to provide services which met specific needs, NATIS continued to strengthen its grip in the following years. The process by which this happened centred on a series of international meetings.

The International Conference on the Development of Documentation and Information Networks in East Africa, held at Nairobi in 1973, was the next major contribution after the Kampala meeting. This conference was held under the auspices of the East African Academy, with the sponsorship of the DSE. It attracted over twenty-five participants including delegates from Kenya, Sudan, Tanzania, Uganda and Zambia. The conference endorsed both the NATIS and

UNISIST programmes that Unesco was at the time promoting and proceeded to recommend that:

> governments of developing countries should urgently formulate national documentation policies and integrate these policies in the national development plans; that each national government should create or cause the creation of an information unit in each ministry, statutory body and other specialized institution, to collect, evaluate, process, and disseminate information in collaboration with a central agency in the same country . . . that a governmental or government chartered body be created to guide, stimulate, and co-ordinate all information services and to establish national information priorities.[10]

As a follow-up to this meeting the DSE proceeded to set in motion a series of 'User Seminars', which they organized and financed. These spanned an eight year period from 1974 to 1981, and covered almost the entire Southern, Central, and Eastern African region, including Sudan (1974), Uganda (1974), Tanzania (1974), Kenya (1975), Zambia (1977), Mauritius (1978), Malawi (1978), Lesotho (1979), Swaziland (1979), Botswana (1980), and Zimbabwe (1981). The object of these seminars was to create a dialogue between librarians and government decision-makers, as well as to raise the consciousness and awareness of these officials of the utility and value of information in the planning and decision-making process. The aim is unimpeachable, but the ethos of these meetings was deeply dependent on the NATIS concept. A final evaluation was conducted in 1981, and we shall consider its findings later in this chapter. For the moment, it is sufficient to note the way in which the seminars consolidated the influence of NATIS.

After Kampala and Nairobi, the next step was a meeting in Brazzaville, People's Republic of Congo. There, in 1976, Unesco convened a NATIS meeting to discuss the planning of documentation and library networks in Africa. In addition to participants from the Congo, delegates arrived from Nigeria, Benin, Togo, Uganda, Senegal, Ivory Coast, Cameroon, Gabon, Tanzania, Ghana, Kenya, and Sierra Leone. The meeting focused on two main issues—the current situation in planning information systems in Africa, and how the recently published NATIS guidelines[11] could be applied within an African context. The first part of the meeting reviewed the progress that had been made since 1970 in implementing the Kampala recommendations. There was very little to report, certainly nothing of a positive nature, and the general opinion appeared to be that if African governments were indeed taking heed of the Kampala recommendations, there was as yet little evidence to confirm this.

Undeterred by this lack of progress, the participants proceeded to review how NATIS guidelines could be used in Africa. Four main areas were dealt with: legislation, creation of co-ordinating bodies, Universal Bibliographic Control, and personnel. The resulting discussion produced twenty-two major recommendations, nine of which were addressed to the Director General of Unesco, and the remainder to member states. Unesco was requested, *inter alia*, to promote postgraduate library education in Africa, to provide a 'massive' number of training scholarships, and to assist in the development of harmonized training programmes in the continent so as to encourage the development of a single unified information profession. Africa's librarians meanwhile were provided with a lengthy list of things to do including:

1. Designing national information policies and incorporating plans for integrated national information systems into national development plans.
2. Profiling user needs and organizing national seminars that would assist in the rapid implementation of NATIS.
3. Strengthening Africa's contribution to Universal Bibliographical Control through legal deposit and the preparation of national bibliographies.
4. Creating additional capacity for the education and training of the continent's librarians, and incorporating into the library education curriculum courses specifically on NATIS.

Fine as these recommendations no doubt sounded at the time, little discussion seems to have taken place as to why nothing had been achieved in the six year period since Kampala. Moreover, virtually no insight is provided in the final report as to how NATIS could be appropriately fashioned to fit in with Africa's development priorities and circumstances. Even more interesting is the fact that NATIS as a separate Unesco programme had less than six months to live. Just over two weeks after the final report of the Brazzaville meeting was published, NATIS was swallowed up by the newly created General Information Programme (PGI), having lost out in its 'battle' with the rival UNISIST programme. Yet, as we shall see, the legacy of NATIS lingered on and continued to dominate Africa's library thinking. Indeed, the belief in its efficacy is as strong now as it was almost twenty years ago.

One would have imagined, almost fifteen years after the Kampala meeting, that either something definite would have emerged, or the entire effort to link integrated library and information systems and national development would have been pronounced a failure and discreetly forgotten. An appropriate point when efforts to promote this approach could have been drawn to a close was provided in 1981. The DSE employed Martin Shio, with the assistance of Augustus Musana, to carry out an evaluation of the user seminars that had been conducted throughout the Southern and Central African region.[12] The purpose of the evaluation was to determine the utility of the seminars in terms of their contribution to increasing the awareness of information as an aspect of planning and decision making.

Shio's investigation, which was an opportunity either to show that there was some strength in the equation, libraries = information = development, or help lay the matter to rest, was a disappointment. The report is vague, inconclusive and lacks the necessary detail which could have settled the issue. He identifies a few initiatives such as the development of the Institute of Southern African Studies in Lesotho, the establishment of the Swaziland National Archives and the setting up of the Zambian National Documentation and Scientific Information Centre, and implies that they were a direct result of the seminars. However, he offers no real evidence that this is actually the case. More telling, perhaps, is the confirmation he provides of the total lack of progress in preparing national information policies, in co-ordinating library and information services, and in developing planning models for integrated library and information services that could be incorporated into national development plans. As these were the priorities identified in Nairobi way back in 1973 when the idea of the user seminars was first mooted, the only conclusion is that up until 1981 there had been no real success.

The DSE, which sponsored the original series of seminars, showed no public sign of dissatisfaction. Furthermore, it was lobbied by librarians from Southern and Central Africa not to discontinue the effort, despite the misgivings implicit in Shio's evaluation report. So there began yet another round of seminars and workshops which commenced with Malawi in 1984 and included Swaziland, Lesotho, Zimbabwe and Botswana, before concluding in Zambia in 1988, when once more an evaluation took place. The objectives of these workshops will no doubt sound familiar, echoing as they do the issues first raised in 1970 in Kampala and resurrected over and over again during the intervening decade or so. Improving planning and decision-making capabilities, assisting socio-economic and cultural development, contributing to national development efforts through the provision of library and information services, sensitizing government officials to the efficacy of information, are all there, and provide a familiar theme that can be traced back to the early 1970s.[13]

Some of the individual papers prepared for this new round of seminars were extremely good, and the reported discussion was very often rich and candid.[14] Difficulties, problems, and failures were all highlighted. For this reason alone, perhaps, this series of seminars was extremely valuable and it is unfortunate that the published volumes of proceedings are not very easily obtainable. Despite these positive aspects, the firm impression that one comes away with, after reading the proceedings, is that little has changed in the twenty years since the original meeting took place in Kampala. The most frequently recurring themes of the final resolutions cover the following areas:

a. information is a pre-requisite to national development, development planning and decision making;
b. developed countries are developed because they are information-rich;
c. Africa is less developed because it is information-poor;
d. as information is the librarians' essential concern, it therefore follows that improved national development will result from more and better libraries and more and better librarians;
e. governments are strongly recommended to legislate for the setting up of national information co-ordinating bodies that will provide the mechanism for the enactment of a national information policy;
f. all types of information service (although usually only libraries are specifically mentioned) should be banded together to form a co-ordinated national information network, that will in turn establish regional and international linkages with other information systems and services.

Why NATIS failed in Africa

Appealing as these ideas sound, there is little evidence that the assumptions so frequently stated have ever been acted upon or the recommendations implemented. Even when claims to progress have been made, they more often than not represent vague hopes rather than operational realities. Over the past few years such concerns have been increasingly widely expressed, although as yet not forcefully enough to dislodge the whole mythology surrounding libraries, information and national development.

The first really serious assault was made in 1979 by Tefko Saracevic (now a library educator at Rutgers University in the USA) when he was commissioned to undertake a study in preparation for the United Nations Conference on Science and Technology and Development.[15] The study attempted to synthesize the perceptions held by information workers, information users, and decision makers in less developed countries, by finding out what they had written about scientific and technical information. Almost from the beginning of his report, Saracevic casts doubt on the authenticity and legitimacy of this written record, describing it as being extremely uneven and pointing out that:

> There is a particularly serious problem with factual evidence on the basis of which statements found in the literature were made, in that the lack of valid and reliable facts, data, statistics, and similar hard evidence in connection with most of the discussions found in the literature on STI [scientific and technical information] in LDCs [less developed countries] is appalling . . . Hundreds of surveys, trip reports and descriptive articles exist on some or other aspect of STI in LDCs; unfortunately many are shallow. This is particularly true of numerous reports done by and for U.N. agencies where trip reports are dubstituted for studies.[16]

Saracevic's critique was subsequently endorsed by Unesco consultant Ulrich Gehrke, who during 1974 advised the Kenyan Government on the establishment of a national information and documentation system.[17] He recounts with wry humour how the rivalry between Unesco's NATIS and UNISIST programmes, which was then at its peak, caused a difficult confrontation between himself and a competing UNISIST consultant:

> In the office of the Unesco science policy adviser attached to the Kenyan Government (Ministry of Finance and Planning) I met another Unesco consultant. He was sent by Unesco-UNISIST, travelling through a number of African countries, including Kenya, reviewing their information facilities and making them acquainted with the aims and advantage of UNISIST. There was considerable overlapping of both missions and they were clearly of a rivaling nature. We had not been informed about each other's mission and we were accordingly astonished. We spontaneously decided not to feel and act as rivals, but to exchange information and experiences and to co-operate amicably during our stay in Kenya. So we did.[18]

He concludes this story by pointing out that Unesco officials back in Paris never adopted the same attitude and the rival protagonists of NATIS and UNISIST continued their battle to the bitter end.

What Saracevic and Gehrke have to say is extremely important for their contributions provide the most convincing clues as to why Africa's library and information services have not yet managed to feature in the development process at a national level. A synthesis of both their arguments proceeds as follows:

• Government officials, planners and decision makers exhibit an extremely low level of awareness with regard to the utility of information, and remain stubbornly unconvinced of its efficacy as a factor in the development process. The necessary conviction that would make NATIS work is not evidenced in the top echelons of government service by the people who hold the purse strings. Neither is information taken seriously at the second tier level of administrators and professionals. It is this category of government employee which one would expect to benefit directly from NATIS-inspired services. In general, however, they rarely utilize information in their day-to-day operations and, more importantly, rarely urge their employers to provide new and improved information services. Even on the rare occasions when a reference to information needs does appear in a planning or policy document, it is no more than a declaration of good intent that is not followed through or supported with the allocation of resources.

• Very few comprehensive national information plans and policies have ever been prepared, and even fewer have been elevated to the extent that they have become an integral part of a national development plan or an essential factor in the planning process. Furthermore, no rationale exists as to why information, rather than housing for example, warrants a separate treatment in national development plans with its own agenda and its own policy formulation. Finally, in the few instances where national information policies and plans have been conceived, no evidence exists that any action has been taken to implement them.

• One of the major impediments to governments' acceptance of NATIS and its associated offerings rests with librarians themselves. The library profession is generally poorly perceived, and the inability of librarians to prepare the necessary project plans that could give effect to NATIS only reinforces this negative perception. While the involvement of librarians in planning national information systems is, on the face of it, not unreasonable, the low esteem in which the profession is held has ensured the non-acceptance of NATIS. Just as librarians bemoan the fact that planners and decision makers show a persistent ignorance of the importance of information as it relates to development, so planners and decision-makers complain that librarians know even less about development issues. Finally, little solace can be found after examining Africa's education and training programmes in library and information studies. They can best be summed up as being deficient, not only in terms of their content, but also in their ability to recruit suitable faculty and students. They are also clearly failing to provide the appropriate preparation to enable the library profession to communicate with planners, decision-makers and high level government officials.

• Existing national information services and systems are usually based on a single, under-resourced, under-staffed, and under-developed 'focal point'. The collection of information resources tends to be confined to a single subject or perhaps a small cluster of subjects, which have little direct relationship to national development priorities. The services offered are rarely matched to actual user needs, and the focal points have never succeeded in gaining a significant niche in the development process at a national level. Librarians talk constantly about co-operative services and networks, but most of what they say is idle rhetoric, for in reality they are defensive, cautious, conservative, and unwilling to risk ceding their tiny under-resourced empires to a larger national system.

• The information collections upon which these national services and systems are based are marginal, inadequate, and over-emphasize bibliographical and referral information at the expense of resources that could provide quick, accurate, and direct answers. Major problems exist with these collections in terms of availability, awareness of their existence, accessibility, selection, the facility to screen, synthesize, and discriminate between various resources, acquisition, accommodation, dissemination, utilization, as well as the application of information technology. All told the majority of these so-called national collections have so many problems that they are unable to provide the solutions that Africa's planners and decision-makers require.

• International and multinational organizations represent the last major piece in the jigsaw which characterizes the failure of integrated library and information systems in Africa. Much of the literature they produce, as well as the studies and consultancies they conduct, are of dubious value. The principal reason for this is that, despite the fact that they are attempting to promote the idea that information is an essential ingredient of planning and decision making, their own reports are virtually devoid of facts and figures upon which informed decisions could be made. Many of these agencies pursue conflicting, contradictory, and uncoordinated programme goals, and often engage in internal or inter-agency feuding at the expense of the development programmes they are supposed to be providing.

This analysis provides a suitable epitaph for this approach to the information needs of Africa. Very little has been achieved from this

preoccupation with integrated plans for library and information services and their relation to national development. Indeed, there is
disenchantment on all sides with the role of libraries. The only positive
effect is that through this disillusionment has emerged a new generation of African librarians who have started to seek their own solutions
and to set their own agenda for the future. Although the first whisper-
ings can be traced back to a minority of the expatriate librarians who
first established Africa's library services, the new voice is essentially a
voice out of Africa itself. It is to what is being said in the 1980s by some
very able and perceptive African librarians that we must turn next.

African librarianship

In 1960 an exchange of correspondence between two of the most
distinguished British expatriate librarians, Wilfred Plumbe and
Ronald Benge, livened up the pages of the *Library Association Record*.
The issue at stake was 'Tropical Librarianship'. Plumbe had argued
that the Library Association (UK) should amend the professional
syllabus and make it more sensitive to the needs of overseas librarians
by including an optional paper which would bear the title 'Tropical
Librarianship'. The amendments he suggested were not intended to
alter in any way the well-established ethos of library service from the
United Kingdom. This, he claimed, was renowned both inside and
outside the British Commonwealth, not only because of its intrinsic
value, but also due to the fact that it "transcends national boundaries
and is undeterred by monsoon rains, desert suns, inefficient postal
services, nationalist fervour, or the hundred and one other obstacles to
study that exist in dozens of countries formerly 'backward' but now
developing with alacrity".[19] Although the content of the envisaged
'Tropical Librarianship' course was not explicitly stated, what
Plumbe obviously had in mind was the inclusion of an element within
the Library Association's syllabus that would enable the 'Tropical
Librarian' to consider these one hundred and one other obstacles
and how they could be overcome in order for the British model of
librarianship to flourish.

Benge, while welcoming the attention that was being paid to
libraries overseas, expressed his misgivings in the following way:

Two recent articles (both by expatriates) have suggested that the L.A.
should invent an examination paper called 'Tropical Librarianship' as if

we suffered from some kind of disease. I am about to propose another paper called 'Temperate Librarianship' which will include questions on whether British librarians should hibernate in the winter. . . . Readers are the key factor in the equation. There is no such thing as a tropical reader. Wilfred Plumbe makes many sound proposals but I detect in several of his articles a suggestion that there is something abnormal about the tropics because it is hot and there are insects and hurricanes. I do not believe that the U.K. is now any kind of norm (if ever it was). (Bethnal Green on a Saturday afternoon in early February has no absolute significance).[20]

At the time of writing Plumbe was at the University of Malaya, and Benge was drawing on his experiences gained in the Eastern Caribbean. The exchange of correspondence converted neither to the other's views. Plumbe in 1987 collected his essays in the book *Tropical Librarianship*.[21] These essays, based on the experiences of his lengthy career in Malaysia, Malawi, Northern Nigeria and elsewhere, present things outside Britain as basically deviations from the norm, which merely call for modifications of British practice.

Benge, after a lengthy sojourn in West Africa, continued to work on his ideas. His book *Cultural crisis and libraries in the third world*[22] provoked considerable interest on publication in 1979, achieved, for a librarianship text, a large circulation and has continued to be read and commented on subsequently. This was an important publication for a number of reasons. The first is that it is one of the few librarianship books that one can confidently recommend as an enjoyable read to the non-librarian. Secondly, Benge recognized that it is more than the obvious physical, environmental, and geographical factors that condition library development in Africa. He avoided any attempt to try to reconcile the differences that do obviously exist between continents with a preconceived world view of librarianship. He recognized that Africa has its own social and cultural values, and took the view that librarianship in Africa should draw inspiration from those values. Benge's clear perceptions and anti-establishment attitudes provided the impetus for what we will refer to as 'African librarianship'.

Those who have sought more worthwhile approaches of this kind have consistently referred back to Benge's work for support, and throughout the 1980s his views have been echoed in numerous conference papers and journal articles. One of the more important was 'On the librarianship of poverty' by Kingo Mchombu, then a training officer with the Tanzania National Library Service and now a lecturer in library studies at the University of Botswana.[23] Mchombu's main argument was that since the foundations of library work in Africa

should be determined by the prevailing social and economic characteristics, then poverty, which was one of the overriding characteristics
of the African environment, required the most positive response from
Africa's librarians and information workers. Over the years since this
article was published, Africa's library profession has begun to absorb
the message and accept the challenge to produce a new library and
information model for the continent.

The main focus of discussion has been the role of libraries in the
rural areas, and the response of librarians to illiteracy. This has
extended to discussion of the means of repackaging information into
forms more appropriate for these purposes, and has to some extent
begun to tackle the issue of the development of a workforce that is
better equipped to establish a redefined library and information
service. As yet, the results of this reformulation have not been fully
articulated. But what has been said has already caused a significant
shift in the subject matter of debate within the African library and
information professions.

The main thread of criticism of established librarianship in Africa
has been directed at its inability to serve those who live in the rural
areas. The argument is that so far Africa's librarians have concentrated their efforts almost exclusively on providing library services to
an urban elite. This has meant the neglect of the information needs of
the rural dwellers who constitute the most severely deprived section of
the continent's population. Two important milestones in the establishment of this argument occurred in the mid-1970s and appeared in
the journal *Rural Africana*. The 1975 issue of this journal looked generally at the problems of communication and information provision in
rural Africa, particularly as they relate to rural development
strategies.[24] At this stage, the library profession seems to have been
seen as having little to offer, but by 1978 an entire special issue[25] was
devoted to the topic of rural library provision. This included a
surprisingly lengthy bibliography showing that Africa's librarians had
been giving thought to this issue for quite some time.

By the beginning of the 1980s a consensus was emerging, amongst
writers on the topic, that there was a need for a new type of library,
offering a radically different approach to library and information provision for rural populations. This new type of institution is seen as
requiring a new paradigm of library service, which would in turn
require a new type of librarian. This new librarian would have to be
endowed with an extended range of skills and competencies far
beyond those normally associated with the library and information

workforce. Despite this tendency towards unanimous acceptance of new rural priorities, the majority of Africa's librarians have been unwilling to venture into the rural areas to put the theories to the test. Fortunately there has been at least one notable exception. This is the University of Ibadan's Rural Development Information System research project (RUDIS) which has been a pathbreaking attempt to move beyond talk to achieve some practical results.[26]

RUDIS commenced in 1981 when a research team under the direction of Olabimpe Aboyade began to visit the village of Badeku near Ibadan offering an informal information service. Though they took with them an initial selection of information materials (pamphlets, posters, audio tapes, etc.), their willingness to listen to the expressed needs of the villagers was their most important contribution. They found a pattern of need for information which largely centred on health, employment, government policies and programmes, and education. Somewhat to the researchers' surprise, the expressed demands of the villagers also included religious and recreational material. In fact, what they were discovering was the need for something much more like 'library' service, albeit library service of a kind rather less sophisticated than that attempted by most national library systems in Africa, than just 'information' service. In Mrs Aboyade's own words, "This is a big reminder that the cultural purposes of a library are not just limited to and appreciated by the leisured and refined members of the society who do not have to spend most of their time working, like rural people, just to make ends meet. Reading (or listening) can play an important role in the beneficial use of leisure, in addition to what rural people normally do to fill their work-free hours."[27]

It is to the project's credit that, although it was set up to consider information needs, the existence of demand for devotional and entertaining materials was not ignored. The researchers attempted to satisfy the whole range of demand, including its unanticipated aspects, with appropriate materials. Reading stories or football match reports aloud to groups was clearly as necessary to the clientele which the project attracted as were posters on making pit latrines or leaflets on farming. The experiment proved quite clearly that rural dwellers will react very favourably to a service which allows them to function as independent information seekers, defining their own needs. For once they were not being seen as passive recipients of official messages or expected to find some mental sustenance in materials chosen for them according to the dictates of established library practice. Their needs

proved to be satisfiable without the usual elaboration of staff, buildings and equipment, that librarians tend to see as essential preconditions of library and information service.

If the RUDIS project had done no more than provide firm evidence
that this approach was effective it would have been a major contribution. The project went much further by providing an outline of what
a rural community library and information service could comprise
and how it could be organized. It must be stressed, however, that it
was only an outline and important questions do remain unanswered.
Badeku is quite near Ibadan and researchers from the library school at
the university there could easily travel to provide the service that was
the central feature of the project. How could practical arrangements
for such a service be sustained in the innumerable much more isolated
villages which are home to so many of Africa's people? The researchers were highly-educated and able people, but could personnel be
found who were capable of replicating elsewhere the services they
provided in Badeku? How would reaction to the service change over
a long period of time? Would take-up of the service grow or decline
once the novelty had gone for both providers and receivers? How
much did the provision of the service to Badeku cost and what would
the provision of service of this type cost if it were provided on an
established basis to other communities? Answers to these and related
questions are needed to confirm whether or not the RUDIS results
are enough, or whether we need to develop ideas on rural services
even further.

In fact, Aboyade has already gone beyond the initial experimentation of RUDIS, to explore the possibilities of extending provision through repackaging of information into a format that would be
more appropriate to the needs of rural dwellers. Translation of
material from English language newspapers, pamphlets, and reference books, and delivering it in the form of audio tapes proved its
worth, as did the recording of radio programmes and material from
books. The latter was then used as the focus for discussion on development issues and concerns. Most interesting of all was the consideration that the project team have given to the use of traditional
communications media, in particular the possibility of using songs,
drama, and the content of traditional festivals to reinforce basic messages and act as a familar medium for communicating 'modern' information.[28] This is an area where the ideas are extremely attractive, but
there has not been nearly enough investigation and experimentation.

At about the same time that RUDIS was being initiated in 1981,

Olabimpe Aboyade was also largely responsible for the organization of a Fédération Internationale de Documentation/Education and Training (FID/ET) Technical Meeting that took place at Ibadan, Nigeria. This also focused on the information needs of non-literate societies. The published proceedings represent Africa's librarians at their best.[29] The papers are, without exception, of an extremely high quality and cover a diverse range of topics, from information provision for rural women to the factors affecting agricultural production amongst Nigeria's non-literate farmers. The opening paper by Olabimpe Aboyade herself[30] and the closing paper by Adetowun Ogunsheye[31] are of particular significance as they highlight two of the essential themes of African librarianship.

The key issue addressed by Aboyade was that of illiteracy, particularly how it affects library provision in rural communities. She puts forward the provocative view that the values generally attached to literacy should not be confined to the ability to read and write. Learning and knowledge are not necessarily synonymous with the written word, and literacy should be considered alongside a range of related, but different, skills which include the ability to interpret visual representations or the ability to use computer programs. How libraries can respond to this more expansive attitude towards literacy is not made clear, but the important point is that the paper presented the development of a new approach to literacy as a fundamental agenda item for Africa's librarians. Ogunsheye's paper brought to the fore the all-important question of the personnel who would operate this new paradigm of library service. In view of the inflexible staffing structures and the inappropriateness of library education curricula that we have already discussed, this is an issue of prime importance to which we will return in the next chapter.

Confirmation that both the subject matter for debate and the underlying assumptions had substantially changed was evidenced in 1986 in Gaborone at the 7th Standing Conference of the Eastern, Central and Southern African Librarians (SCECSAL VII). The conference was divided into three main parts: a pre-conference workshop dealing with repackaging of information for illiterate users, the main conference which was concerned with libraries and literacy, and a post-conference seminar which looked at education and training of the library and information workforce. Once again the published proceedings are of an extremely high quality and provide testimony to the new spirit in Africa's library profession.[32] Treating the three inter-linked parts of the conference as a whole the ideas that emerged witnessed a remarkable consensus as to the priorities. These can be itemized as follows:

   a. the rural areas were perceived as having absolute priority;
   b. the illiterate majority formed the target group for service in the rural areas;
   c. information that had been re-packaged in a form more appropriate to the needs of a mainly non-literate clientele, and made available through media more in tune with their existing modes of communication, was to be the focus of resource provision;
   d. a new and quite different attitude to librarianship had to be fostered, emphasizing new skills and competencies, to offer this new concept of library service.

SCECSAL VII was important since it confirmed that librarians from the Eastern side of the continent were moving in the same direction as their West African colleagues, who had been somewhat more advanced along these lines. It also provided a good synthesis of the new directions in which Africa's librarianship is proceeding.

Conclusion

Africa's librarians were not slow in recognizing that the failures of their services in the years after independence threatened a dismal fate. They had to counter the negative perception of their work and once again convince Africa's governments that libraries did have a role to play for the nation. The initial strategy they adopted to achieve this was that of attempting to argue a direct link between libraries and national development through the provision of integrated library and information services. Almost twenty years of deliberations on this issue clearly failed to produce any positive results. In response to this failure came the re-evaluation we have just described.

The new African librarianship, recognizing the lessons of poverty and of the failure of existing library and information orthodoxies to flourish in African conditions, has shifted the emphasis of attention towards the rural, illiterate population, but as yet has few results to show. The evidence of its existence is chiefly to be found in journal articles, conference papers and research reports. What has been written and said holds considerable promise for the future of Africa's libraries and the continent's information environment, but until practical results can be shown, the prospect that it, like the NATIS approach, may in the end achieve nothing is a real one. Despite such fears, the approach is managing to attract a growing body of support amongst library and information personnel. If its supporters can succeed in persuading governments to adopt proposals for new services and if these achieve some worthwhile results, then the regeneration of librarianship in an African form will begin to be a reality.

Our concern about this approach is that it does not as yet provide a complete agenda for the future of library and information work in Africa. It has so far almost totally ignored information provision to Africa's teeming urban areas; nor has it had anything to say about the library and information needs of Africa's huge school-going population; and finally it has failed to provide an effective synthesis between the information needs of rural illiterate populations and the obviously different but equally valid information requirements of the educated urban elite. In the next chapter we will suggest our own slightly different set of priorities, developed out of the same analysis, but restoring a little of the missing balance.

References

1. Durrani, S. Rural information in Kenya. *Information Development*, 1, 1985. p 152.
2. Tocatlian, J. *and* Abid, A. The development of library and information services in developing countries: Unesco/PGI's role and activities. *IFLA Journal*, 12, 1986. p 281.
3. Parker, J.S. *Unesco and library development planning*. London, Library Association, 1985.
4. Liebaers, H. *Mostly in the line of duty: thirty years with books*. The Hague, Martinus Nijhoff, 1980. p 63.
5. Harrison, K.C. *Republic of the Seychelles: libraries, documentation and archives services*. Paris, Unesco, 1978.
6. Unesco. Expert Meeting on National Planning of Documentation and Library Services in Africa, Kampala, Uganda, 7-15 December, 1970. *Final Report*. Paris, Unesco, 1971.
7. Parker, J.S. *op. cit.* pp 227-231.
8. Kaungamno, E.E. *Books build nations: Vol. 2. Library services in Tanzania*. London and Dar es Salaam: Transafrica/TLS, 1979. pp 24-25.
9. Parker, J.S. *op. cit.* pp 230-231.
10. Conference on Information Networks in East Africa, 1973. *Unesco Bulletin for Libraries*, 28, 1974. p 52.
11. Unesco. Meeting of experts on planning documentation and library networks in Africa (NATIS), Brazzaville, People's Republic of Congo, 5-10 July 1976. *Final Report*. Paris: Unesco, 1976. p 1.

12. Shio, M.J. *and* Musana, A. *Evaluation of user seminars conducted in Tanzania, Zambia, Malawi, Lesotho, Swaziland, Botswana.* Bonn, DSE, 1981.

13. Huttemann, L. *ed. Establishment, function and management of a national library and documentation service.* (Harare Workshop Papers) Bonn, DSE, 1985.

14. Huttemann, L. *ed. Establishment and management of a national information service in Botswana.* (Gaborone Workshop Papers). Bonn/Gaborone, DSE/Botswana National Library Service, 1987.

15. Saracevic, T. Perception of the needs for scientific and technical information in less developed countries. *Journal of Documentation*, 36, 1980. 214–267.

16. Saracevic, T. *op. cit.* p 216.

17. Gehrke, U. Information for development. Some problems of national co-ordination, regional co-ordination and international assistance. *INSPEL.* 19, 1985. 166–198.

18. Gehrke, U. *op. cit.* pp 174–175.

19. Plumbe, W.J. British librarianship overseas. *Library Association Record.* 62, 1960. 272.

20. Benge, R.C. An expatriate in an emergent country. *Library Association Record*, 63, 1961. 333.

21. Plumbe, W.J. *Tropical Librarianship.* Metuchen, N.J., Scarecrow Press, 1988.

22. Benge, R.C. *Cultural crisis and libraries in the third world.* London, Bingley, 1979.

23. Mchombu, K.J. On the librarianship of poverty. *Libri*, 32, 1982. 241–250.

24. Opubor, A.E. *ed. Rural Africana.* (Issue on communication for rural development) 27, 1975.

25. *Rural Africana.* (New Series) 1, 1978.

26. Aboyade, B.O. Communications potentials of the library for non-literates—an experiment in providing information services in a rural setting. *Libri*, 34, 1984. 243–262.

27. *Ibid.* p 259.

28. Aboyade, B.O. *The provision of information for rural development.* Ibadan, Fountain Publications, 1987.

29. Aboyade, B.O. *ed. Education and training for library and information services in a predominantly non-literate society.* The Hague, FID, 1981.

30. Aboyade, B.O. Communication and transfer of information in non-literate societies. *In*: Aboyade, B.O. *Education and training . . . op. cit.* pp 13–21.

31. Ogunsheye, F.A. Education and training for library and information services to rural communities. *In*: Aboyade, B.O. *Education and training . . . op. cit.* pp 87–103.

32. Asamani, J.O. *and others eds. Libraries and Literacy. Proceedings of the 7th Standing Conference of the Eastern, Central and Southern African Librarians, Gaborone, 4–8 Aug, 1986.* Gaborone, Botswana Library Association, 1987.

Chapter Five

A Foundation for the Future

Introduction

In moments of despair the question, 'Is there any future for library and information work in Africa?' must have occurred to most of its practitioners. Even the casual observer of Africa's library scene would find it difficult not to provide the most obvious answer—'No!' The achievements of library pioneers in the first years of independence provided a beginning, but left a flawed legacy and a sizeable agenda of expansion, improvement and re-definition which has not yet been achieved. The effect of the national and continental crises that have bedevilled Africa's economies over the last few decades has not been conducive to the development of library and information services. Even so, the problem with Africa's libraries is more fundamental and more deeply-rooted than the lack of financial resources, for even if library budgets were to be magically sated with an overflow of money, the crisis would still remain. In fact, it would probably be exacerbated as Africa's librarians started to puzzle how they could spend their new-found fortunes.

The essential problems have been a lack of vision and an obsession with a foreign library ethos that, as far as Africa is concerned, is largely bankrupt. There is a tendency to focus attention on the immediate day-to-day routine problems which tends to exclude the contemplation of longer-term prospects and possibilities. Too many solutions have been sought through conventional library methods, which have been found wanting when applied in an African context. Also, too many features which are typical of Africa's information environment have either been ignored, or perceived as obstacles that

119

must be eradicated before libraries can flourish. Only rarely have Africa's librarians viewed their immediate information environment in a positive light, to determine what attributes it possesses and how they can be harnessed to provide the ingredients of an African library ethos and an African library service which clearly attempts to meet Africa's information needs.

Yet if, as we believe, there *is* a future for library and information work in Africa, in which direction does that future lie and what changes if any does it require? The first pointers to the direction for the future have already been provided by those whose ideas have been characterized as 'African librarianship'. The major preoccupation of this emerging library ethos has been to reconstruct the principles usually felt to govern the provision of library and information service so as to match them with the needs of societies which have low levels of literacy. It is an attempt to shift the emphasis away from service to the literate minority and focus service priorities on the illiterate or semi-literate majority. This 'African librarianship', and the points of view it represents, undoubtedly sets the mood and provides some of the substance for Africa's library future. Nevertheless 'African librarianship' as presently conceived is limited, and should only form a part, albeit a major one, of the structure of a possible future for librarianship in Africa.

The major defect in 'African librarianship' is not fundamental, but is essentially one of scope. In a reaction to existing imbalances in the provision of library services within African countries, advocates of 'African librarianship' swing towards an equally unbalanced vision of information provision. There is a failure to consider the continent's information environment as an organic whole, with legitimate needs at all economic and educational levels requiring the provision of service either immediately or at some subsequent planning stage. In order to provide what we consider to be a firmer foundation for library development in Africa we intend to outline the basis of a broader vision. This will involve an examination of how applicable the approaches adopted by those who have argued for 'African librarianship' are to a broader spectrum of the continent's information users.

Following Mchombu's precept we will begin with the assumption that librarianship for Africa must take the inescapable reality of poverty as its central preoccupation. This does not mean just the financial poverty experienced by institutions, which limits the number and scope of library and information projects, but also poverty as the main fact in the lives of the great majority of potential and actual beneficiaries of services. It also means poverty in the literacy skills that have to be assumed to exist before the practice of traditional librarianship can be pursued. We do not, however, assume that shortage of money, scarcity of literacy, or impoverishment of the conventional booktrades necessarily either rule out some kind of information service, or dictate that services should be confined to a minority who can afford and make use of the usually accepted forms of provision.

Realism on the issue of poverty points to the need for a rigorous assessment of priorities. This inevitably means that we will suggest that some treasured aspects of service must be scaled down at present, or even temporarily abandoned and relegated to the status of long-term planning possibilities. It also means that we will suggest that enhanced versions of some existing services will be necessary. Most significant of all, it means creating new services. Although we will talk of the usefulness of repackaging (in terms of the work that can be done on information to make it usable by the African citizen) our concern is less with the repackaging of services, or even with the repackaging of personnel, than with making fresh services, staffed by new information professionals. Such services we see as a major contribution to a self-reliant Africa. The services must emerge from Africa's own resources and relate to the continent's peculiar needs. Self-reliance in information is all of a piece with economic, cultural and political self-reliance.

A new library and information paradigm, based on the recognition that poverty dictates a revision of priorities, and guided by the principle that self-reliance is all-important, has to be rooted in clear ideas about users and potential users of information. There has been precious little serious investigation or published research which throws light on the relation of African citizens to formal information systems. As Ndiaye suggests, "The librarian's job is to try to gain in-depth knowledge of orality in order to mark out the areas where there is conflict and those where orality and libraries are really compatible. The needs of both must be brought into harmony. The effectiveness of libraries is at stake in all the regions where books are today being introduced, and where the population is acutely aware of their value and necessity".[1]

Examination of the oral medium shows the African populace as enthusiastic handlers of information via traditional channels. In particular, Aboyade's revealing accounts of information use in a rural Nigerian village provide an awareness of different categories of information need. Some studies, notably those of Aiyepeku[2] provide the first real shreds of evidence of information use by researchers and government officials. These few examples, however, represent a major part of the very small body of systematic knowledge assembled by the library and information community on how information is used in Africa. Sociologists and communication studies scholars have rather more frequently pursued relevant investigations.[3] The sad thing is that one can find little evidence, from citations or allusions in the library and information literature, that their work is known to library and information workers. In sum, the available information is small in bulk and some of it has had no discernible impact on the information professions. Altogether, this information is scarcely sufficient to start to answer the questions we raised at the beginning of this book, 'What do the people know, and how do they know it?'

Africa's potential and current library and information users are generally assumed to fall into one or other of two groups as follows:

a. *Illiterate rural farmers* who can boast little formal education and whose information needs have generally been ignored by librarians. These information needs, which embrace such topics as health, hygiene, soil conservation, crop husbandry, child rearing, and family welfare, are justly perceived as pressing in the most urgent degree.

b. *Literate urban elites* who are generally highly educated, who represent only a tiny minority of Africa's population and whose information needs are, in theory, well provided for through the network of library services that have been created throughout Africa since the early days of independence. They have generally been categorized as a section of the population which should present few, if any, difficulties in terms of information provision, despite their evident refusal to make full use of what has already been provided for them.

While this may be an over-simplification of the approach which Africa's librarians adopt towards their potential clientele, it does reflect many of the opinions that can be found in the recent literature. Since professional efforts have hitherto been directed much more towards the literate elite, it is not surprising that the primary objective is now increasingly seen as coming to terms with the problems created by illiteracy. Illiteracy has, indeed, been condemned by African librarians as the "scourge, menace, humiliation, enemy number one, the worst evil of the human race and other dismal but apt phrases".[4] The increased emphasis on working with the illiterate rural poor is not one which we would wish to challenge, but arguments for this approach do seem to represent the population as much too neatly divided into mutually exclusive groups. The dividing line often seems to be drawn more or less according to where the potential user is situated, with the rural dweller being assumed to be illiterate and the urban citizen to be literate. This is an assumption that does not stand up to analysis. A rural-illiterate, urban-literate equation is much too simple. In particular, it neglects the migrant population of the shanty towns, who despite their physical proximity to educational and information facilities, may in many ways be as deprived as the rural poor.

What is more, this approach involves a very limited version of literacy and what it really means. Literacy is a magical word, laden with strong positive connotations, implying the highest and purest standards, and bestowing a mark of civilization on those who are in possession of it. The converse is also true, for to call someone, or their work, illiterate, is to express outright and sneering contempt. To the question 'Is literacy truly important?' the answer would generally be that it is *all*-important: knowledge, education, culture, good citizenship, material and spiritual success all spring from it. Without literacy no one can properly function in society, compete for well-paid and fulfilling jobs, or contribute to the political and social life of the community. It naturally follows that those who cannot read and write are condemned to be marginal in terms of their contribution to society. In the industrialized countries the literate person can easily forget what a hard-won skill literacy is and talk as though literacy is a normal state, to which non-literate people are exceptions. Even in Africa, where this is patently not the case, there is a tendency to adopt a similar attitude and neglect the needs of the non-literate majority.

Faced with the assumptions and prejudices surrounding the word and the image it portrays, thoughtful and radical discussion of literacy is not easy. This is especially so in the context of the oral societies of Africa, where the values implicit in the Western use of the word do not apply. Any rational discussion of libraries and literacy must therefore attempt the difficult task of breaking some of the taboos which have largely remained unquestioned or have been ignored by most commentators.

African history brings the problem into sharp focus for although archaeological evidence suggests that in the Stone Age, Africa was more advanced technologically than Europe or Asia, this lead was very clearly lost in the subsequent ages. This, it has been suggested, was because Africa did not invent its own art of writing.[5] This resulted in an almost total dependence on human memory, meaning that the would-be innovator had too frequently to start from first principles, with an incomplete and imperfect knowledge of the work of others. Knowledge was likely to be imperfect because of the physical limits of memory, the tendency of information held in the human mind to be modified with the passage of time, the loss of that knowledge due to the mortality of the human carrier, and the lack of access to that knowledge due to the inability of the human carrier to be in more than one place at the same time. Accepting that the risks associated with the first of these two points can be exaggerated, the second two cannot be avoided and are inherent defects in any mode of oral communication.

It can be argued further that, as a result, not only did Africa stagnate technologically, but its lack of written record made it more vulnerable to the depradations of Europeans and Arabs. These intruders, in justifying their actions to themselves and others, were able to disregard the culture and achievements of Africa, because of the insubstantial formal record. They could claim that they were providing something (civilization, economic order, religious faith) where there was nothing. This is indeed the type of viewpoint that outsiders (explorers, colonialists and missionaries) brought to Africa. They tended to see the continent south of the Sahara as benighted in various ways, among which the absence of literacy was prominent. Africans could consequently be carried off into slavery, taxed, ruled, evangelized, or employed as lowly producers of primary commodities for the economies of the northern hemisphere. In addition the outsiders could attempt to alter African people's own perception of what had happened by superimposing the power of their own written versions of history of the continent on the Africans' own more fragile, orally-transmitted versions. This they did with some success.

That there is truth in this analysis of the way in which the absence of literacy contributed to Africa's tragedies is hard to deny, but it is a Eurocentric view and a thoroughly unhelpful starting point in dealing with the question of the significance of literacy. In the first place, the conclusion that it is the lack of a written record that has inhibited the development of Africa is not necessarily correct. The level of development that can be achieved without the written record has never been fully tested and, more crucially, the level of achievement of oral societies never fully recognized. For example, the complex and advanced society which built Great Zimbabwe is only known by vague and unreliable mentions in the chronicles of outside travellers, and from the much-damaged archaeological evidence to be found at the ruins of Great Zimbabwe itself. A vast complex extending over sixty acres, dating back in its earliest parts to the 8th century AD, comprising an imposing structure of stone walls held together without the aid of mortar and made habitable by a complex pattern of drainage, Great Zimbabwe represents a magnificent symbol of the great inland empire that was then ruled by the Karanga-speaking peoples of what is now south-east Zimbabwe. The lack of a written record made possible the often ludicrous, but widely published, efforts of Rhodesian colonists and their apologists to attribute the building of Great Zimbabwe to any civilization, be it Hebrew, Phoenician, Arab, Indian, Greek, or Roman, rather than admit its true African origins.

Alternative explanations of why such promising societies as that which built Great Zimbabwe failed to progress and of why Africa was so vulnerable to outside domination are not lacking. To take just one example, it is possible to explain much by the concept of isolation. Over large parts of the continent's surface, the simple matter of moving from one area to another is, in fact, not simple at all. Surface geology and climate have produced arid semi-desert in the north and centre; there are high ranges of mountains; and there is dense jungle in the west and in the Zaire basin. All of these have presented serious barriers to travel. Rivers, which in other continents facilitate movement, in Africa leave the high central plains over impassable rapids and falls. Disease, mainly in the form of insect-carried sicknesses such as malaria and sleeping sickness, again has restricted the movement of people. The latter, in particular, because it afflicts draught animals, has inhibited human movement very severely. Population was, in many parts of the continent, very thinly scattered and those concentrations of people which did exist were often isolated from each other. Languages and dialects multiplied under these circumstances. Strong states that could resist outside aggression tended to form with difficulty and disintegrate with ease. Without regular contact between groups of people trade in the objects of material culture, which has contributed so much to the economic welfare of other parts of the world, has not been easy. The cultural cross-fertilization that has so often been of central importance to the growth of civilizations, was also often limited by the difficulties of travel. Innovation and sustained development were thus very often inhibited by the isolation of cultural and linguistic communities from each other.

By emphasizing the significance of a factor such as isolation in the success and failure of past societies it is possible to counterbalance the contemporary preoccupation with literacy. This is important in this context, because the emphasis on literacy has led to the consistent undervaluing of oral society. Although later in this chapter we will discuss the important work that libraries must do in relation to literacy programmes, our contention is that the emphasis on information institutions as services to the literate is very limiting. A more appropriate approach than an exclusive concentration on serving those who can read, or who are learning to read, is to take oral society as one of the constant and positive factors in the information environment. This would mean wholehearted acceptance of the necessity for library and information service to all potential users, whether or not they can read or write.

The basic assumption would be that every citizen is either formally literate or has some equivalent set of skills which enables them to function in society and the economy. The precise form that the provision of information and library services to specific communities would take, would then follow from the balance of skills available in those communities. Thus a university library or an information service to senior government employees could proceed on the assumption of the highest levels of literacy skills, whilst at the other extreme, service in a very isolated rural community might reasonably be provided on the assumption of an almost complete reliance on oral communication. Naturally, service at these two extremes would take forms which differed in the most extreme ways.

This expansion of the definition of the potential community for library and information service does not change the need for decisions over priorities. Indeed, it increases the urgency for clear decisions, since it calls for the allocation of the very scarce resources available for information purposes across a wider range of possibilities for service. In the light of this, it is our belief that three main areas for the concentration of effort can be identified.

We see the first of these priorities as service to that considerable section of the population which has its equivalent of literacy through its use of what has been referred to as 'Oramedia'.[6] This oral society, urban or rural, presents the most fascinating and difficult challenges, but the responsibility to contribute to its information activity is clear and urgent. Secondly, it is necessary to focus on that growing sector of society which is passing through the various stages of acquiring the skills of reading and writing, and putting them to use in education. Thirdly, those who have already reached the stage at which they are able to make clear and specific demands for information of specialized and complex kinds deserve immediate consideration. This group presents some of the most difficult decisions over priorities, because the materials which they may need are the most difficult and expensive to obtain. Each of these groups will be discussed separately in what follows, but we have to point out that this particular choice of priorities leaves little space for many of the traditional functions of national and public library systems. The model we will present ignores many types of service and calls for new attitudes towards institutions.

Information and oramedia

The ways in which the oral tradition can be integrated with information and even library service are illustrated to some extent by the story of Odi Weavers in Botswana, which was first told in 1977.[7] The small rural factory called 'Lentswe la Odi Weavers' produces woven tapestries, wall hangings and carpets, using traditional patterns and themes from the weavers' experience. The factory started operations in the early 1970s with the primary intention of providing employment for the Odi villagers, enabling at least some of them to break free from their subsistence livelihood.

The theme for each tapestry is selected and discussed by the weavers before even a single thread is woven. The process has been described in the following way:

> Themes are drawn from real incidents in the women's lives, current events in the newspaper or radio, traditional stories, arguments or issues which come up in their daily work and topics of conversation in the village. For example one weaving came out of discussion on a self-help project to build a drift across the Oodi river. When this work project was organised, only the weavers and the poorer members of the community participated. The richer villagers, who stood to benefit more from the project, refused to help. This issue created a lot of discussion and inspired a weaving which was later used to initiate public discussion within the village as a whole. An example of another source was a story in the newspaper about Zimbabwean children fleeing Smith's troops and crossing the border into Botswana. This caught the women's interest and inspired another weaving. A third example is a question one woman raised: 'What is FRELIMO? Is it a football team?' This led to a long discussion about the liberation struggles in southern Africa and several weavings on this theme.[8]

The whole process is then repeated when the weaving is finished with the completed tapestry being hung for display in a central meeting place, providing a powerful visual focus for more discussion, debate and dialogue. The tapestries and the process by which they are designed and produced thus provide a highly potent medium through which important information is communicated and disseminated.

The relationship between work and traditional modes of information transfer also assisted the weavers in solving some of the day-to-day problems that arose at the factory. Originally the factory operated as a co-operative in which everyone shared in the decision making. Even the tasks usually associated with management, such as budgeting, book-keeping, stock control, purchasing and marketing, were carried out on a rotational basis with each weaver having the opportunity to acquire these various skills. Gradually, as the factory grew and became more successful, this co-operative mechanism was replaced by a management committee which took a firmer control of the day-to-day running of the factory, and the former system of rotating tasks was no longer adhered to. The weavers began to feel that the management was developing elitist tendencies. The first thing the weavers did in order to indicate their discontent was to compose a song—'We're so cold working in the factory but the management are enjoying themselves sitting outside in the sun'. One group went a stage further and staged a drama in the village which depicted the change in worker-management relationships that had resulted from the move from a co-operative sharing approach to management by committee. On the basis of these expressions of their grievances, the workers eventually resolved the difficulties to their satisfaction.

As the profits from the weaving factory grew, so the weavers decided to establish a development fund—'Sethunya sa Ditlhabololo' (Flower of Development)—which would provide loans and grants to other groups and individuals to establish small-scale projects related to economic production. The methods adopted by the weavers to promote the fund drew on their experiences in the labour dispute, but also expanded the range of forms of communication used. The traditional village court, the *kgotla*, was exploited as a forum for publicity. Tapestry exhibitions and the presentation of dramas were used to explain the fund in nearby villages. Gradually takers emerged, and new businesses were set up using funds from Odi.

This example of how traditional non-print media and modes of communication can be used to generate and disseminate information may not appear at first glance to fall within the sphere of interest of the library profession. It is, however, precisely because such methods are unfamiliar and do not fit within accepted definitions of the concerns of information workers, that they are so important. By understanding oramedia and learning how to use them, the information worker has the potential to perform a useful function in parts of society usually untouched by conventional services. Indeed as Adimorah puts it, "Instead of playing an active role as change agents, most of these libraries play an information suppressing role to their community in failing to disseminate information geared towards bettering the lot of the rural poor. The public libraries still lack the interest or capacity for carrying out an analysis of the community, isolating its needs and satisfying them".[9] The question remains, however, as to just how this can be achieved. Few practical examples are available to answer this.

Current thinking on the response to oramedia has tended to focus on the capture by a conventional library or archive service of the oral tradition and its repackaging in audio-visual formats. As long ago as 1973, in a contribution to a conference on publishing in Africa, K.K. Oyeoku suggested that "The initial emphasis of African libraries need not be on the printed word. It is quite feasible and more meaningful to start a library in a rural community with miles of tapes of the people's folklore, music and culture".[10] He proposed experimentation with a new institution in a rural village, which would collect oral material from the villagers into a community library of tapes. The institution would gradually transcribe the material for use in connection with literacy teaching, so that new readers were dealing with familiar and well-loved material. Second and third stages would involve local preparation and informal publishing of primary and vocational education materials developed from the oral materials and using the skills acquired during that stage of the programme. A final fourth stage, of publishing for secondary and higher education and for other purposes, including recreation, could then be explored, forming the basis of a sound library collection. Mali has possibly been at the forefront in exploring such possibilities and it is there we must turn for an example.

The plan to harness Mali's oral tradition and then to make it available in libraries in the form of sound tapes has been described by Majid Rahnema, who at the time the project was being formulated in 1982 was the Resident Representative of the United Nations Development Programme (UNDP) in Mali. The sound library scheme was conceived as a joint UNDP/Malian Government project, and involved the establishment of a headquarters sound library at Bamako, the capital, with each village having its own branch which would make available on tape the local communities' oral heritage and tradition. The operation would then be extended to remoter rural areas through the use of a mobile sound library incorporated into the existing traditional mobile library service. As depicted by Rahnema the village sound libraries would be:

> designed as autonomous centres of living culture in which information can be collected and exchanged, primarily for the large majority who are still illiterate. Thus instead of being isolated in their illiteracy, they will, by means of recorded items, be able to acquire vivifying information on their own culture, as well as that of neighbouring socio-cultural communities and other countries throughout the world.
>
> They will be a new kind of library equipped with the basic technical means for making and storing tape-recordings, so that anyone can come and obtain information on a variety of subjects such as the history of the village, general history, traditional technical skills, appropriate technology, elementary health care, agriculture, animal husbandry, etc. They will function like ordinary libraries but with sound recordings in the place of books and will have facilities for borrowing, listening to and copying tapes.[11]

The reponse to the idea of these sound libraries, both at government level and amongst the inhabitants of the rural villages that were selected to participate in the experimental pilot project was, according to Rahnema, one of excitement and enthusiasm. Whilst it would be churlish not to be enthusiastic about such a proposal, it does not present the wholly convincing argument that Rahnema would obviously like us to accept.

The main criticism is that, despite the appearance of a new approach, the sound libraries, as described, are still firmly rooted in the traditions of book librarianship. The approach fails to accept oramedia as a valid mode of communication that can contribute without having to be legitimized by a modern format. In addition, the whole notion of recording oral tradition and depositing the tapes in a conventional library setting presupposes that those for whom this service was ostensibly intended, Mali's rural villagers, do, once the initial enthusiasm has died down, have the need or desire for such a service. Historians, social anthropologists and musicologists would certainly value its content very highly, but whether it is the only, or most appropriate, response to the oral tradition is open to debate. If the villagers do prove to have a sustained enthusiasm for the service, there are still problems. The idea of transmuting the oral record so that it can be heard on tape or cassette creates yet another instance of technological dependence.

Cassette players are expensive in village terms, there are no facilities for repair, and tapes are vulnerable and shortlived. Although the sound library idea offers immediate benefits, in the long term it enmeshes the oral medium in technological limitations that are not intrinsic to the medium itself. The essence of the oral tradition is that it lives and breathes, as a living organism. Recording technology may ultimately inhibit its growth and development by freezing performances in a profoundly untraditional fashion. Once committed to tape, or even worse transcribed to form a written record, many of the added nuances and the adaptability of the forms that are an essential part of the oral medium disappear and thus much of the original message is lost. These criticisms do not invalidate the sound library as a contribution to new forms of information service, but merely place it in proportion to other types of contribution.

These other types of contribution are not really to be found in the literature of librarianship. It is to the literature on non-formal education that we must turn in order to obtain a clearer perception of possibilities. Within Third World countries there has been, during the last ten years or so, a growing interest in the indigenization of non-formal education so that it can become more closely integrated within the fabric of society. The ensuing debate has created a polarization of differing approaches which have been labelled as 'reformist/instrumentalist' and 'popular education/structuralist.' Both are in basic agreement that traditional media have an important part to play in development, but differ as to the precise role that those media should play in the development process. One approach views them as merely a tool to make government development programmes more effective. The other perceives the oral medium as the one authentic voice of the community, through which various strategies and options for development should be allowed to emerge without any outside interference, which could affect not only what is said but also the medium through which it is transmitted.[12]

The reformist/instrumentalist position is basically that which is represented in the attempt to inform or propagandize via services such as agricultural extension, radio programmes, or government printing and publishing of information materials. The conventional library can very obviously be made part of such an approach. In something like the RUDIS project, even though the initiative came from the research team, the approach is responsive and reactive to local needs in a way more in tune with the popular education/structuralist approach. The Malian sound libraries, by seeking to capture the oral tradition and making it more widely available, take this approach even further. Our feeling is that the lessons for library and information service to be derived from this approach can be taken even further, removing the focus of service from a reading room, sound library, culture house or conventional book-based library to a variety of less formal settings. Indeed, it is possible to envisage aspects of service also detached, to a considerable extent, from reliance on the information resources, such as books, tapes, slides, films and so on, which are normally associated with such structures.

Service provided by an individual best described as an 'information animator' would take the popular education/structuralist approach and integrate it fully with the ultimate aims of library and information service. Although this is virtually a new concept the functions are incidentally performed to an extent by certain members of society such as chiefs, school teachers or Catholic priests, who, it has been claimed, are "part and parcel of an extension of the community information network".[13] The story of the Odi weavers indicates the kinds of benefits that can be obtained by communities which have better access to and control of information. From the accounts available of what happened at Odi it is not possible to tell whether any particular individual acted as a catalyst in the weavers' use of song and story, but we feel that if such an individual could be made available, then much could be done to stimulate the information activities of suitable communities. By 'suitable', we mean communities that as yet have few or no formal information services available to them and where it could reasonably be predicted that a conventional library service would find few users even if it were to be provided.

Information animators would best be employed by an agency, such as a national library service or a department of adult education, though they could also form a separate service, liaising with established services. Recruiting for such a service would not be easy, for, whilst candidates would need a wide range of talents, there could not be a career structure offering a long series of promotion steps. Animators would probably need to be young professionals from adult education and information professions who would subsequently go on to develop careers in other aspects of those professions. Ideally they would work themselves out of a job, by stimulating local information activity to such an extent that the communities in which they worked could support more formal institutions.

The locations in which they would work could be both rural villages and urban slums or shanty towns. Although the latter display aspects of modernity, they still also exhibit many of the characteristics of their rural counterparts, including the transmission of information through oramedia. The animator's working day would not be tied to an office, though some base would be needed. This could be provided by almost any local institution that had a room available to loan or let. There would also be the need for close relations with a variety of institutions, for example, in urban areas, self-help housing agencies, adult education centres or night schools, churches, or financial and mutual aid institutions such as burial societies, and in rural settings, village co-operatives, schools, or the traditional courts. These institutions, or even the informal meeting places where people gather to talk over the business of the day when dark is falling, would be the sites for informal surgeries, at which the animator could explore the information needs of individuals and groups. Such occasions could also be opportunities to discuss and interpret the content of broadcasting and newspapers.

Shiraz Durrani makes the intriguing suggestion that the village food kiosks, found in Kenya and other countries, provide an ideal focus for this type of informal information service.[14] They frequently have radios, cassette players, and even TV sets for their customers. Their walls carry pictures and posters, customers read aloud to others from newspapers, and there is naturally plentiful exchange of facts and opinion between owners and customers. In general terms, bases for the work of the animator will depend on where the people can be encountered in a particular community, and there is no lack of such opportunities.

The information resources that the animator would use to meet the needs which emerge from such encounters might well be in documentary form. They could be leaflets prepared by extension services and other government agencies, publications obtained from a variety of library services, or material from newspapers and magazines. The main task would be that of mediating between the content of these resources and the oral medium in which much of the material would be delivered. This delivery would not only involve the passing on of answers to specific questions, but contributing to the incorporation of information of general interest, on such topics as health and hygiene, farming, child-rearing, or education, into the framework of traditional narrative, song, drama and festivals, as suggested by Aboyade.[15] The animator would not only repackage information in this way, but be an interpreter of the information, aiding the individual in absorbing and using it. In the reverse direction the animator should be able to contribute to the repackaging of traditional content, in forms such as audio or video tape, and print, as discussed earlier in this chapter. In this way the messages of oral society would be made open to a wider audience, and the voice of the underprivileged made audible outside the immediate community. The animator would also be available to advise other agencies and services on the delivery of their information, and the obtaining of feedback from their clientele.

Explorations of the principles behind the concept of the information animator can be found in various parts of Africa. For instance in Kenya, the National Committee on Utilisation of Science and Technology looked at the dissemination of research results to the farmer.[16] They came to realize that one-way flows of information from the researcher to the farmer, via the extension services, were providing messages which were too technical and insufficiently related to the farmers' objectives and resources. They proposed a 'brokerage model' which incorporated first the input of farmers' ideas and knowledge to the research design process, and then the assessment of programmes in the light of feedback from the farmers. They concluded that the media to be used in this needed to be as informal as possible, since the use of glossy brochures and expensively-produced films rigidified the communication from the research centres and detracted from the interaction which was sought.

It is also true that the conclusion that traditional media should play a large part in information systems is not a unique one. People working in the discipline of communication studies, such as Kwame Boafo, have discussed ideas of precisely this type. He, for instance, argues that "An optimal information utilisation in rural development in Africa is dependent on communication strategies which consistently amalgamate the traditional media and the modern media technologies into adequate channels for horizontal and vertical information flows in the rural communities".[17] Experiments conducted in Nigeria in the early 1970s by Fiofori showed that people happily accepted the use of oral narratives to convey modern messages adjusting easily to new content in old forms. The familiarity of the narrator and the form of the narration, in conjunction with the potential for dialogue, were the strengths of this technique which he called 'communoraldition'.[18]

As we have suggested, the written word would undoubtedly play a part in the animator's activities, first of all as the source for information to be delivered in other, more traditional, forms, but gradually as an increasingly important method of delivery in its own right. The penetration of traditional society that written communication has already achieved, and the near certainty of the increase of that penetration, must not be forgotten in the shift of emphasis towards oramedia. The villagers of Dome in Ghana told investigators that they had used printed information to help them both to learn practical skills like rabbit keeping, pottery, and lock repairs, and for information about the history of their country. Indeed "almost every house which the interviewers visited had a few books or magazines".[19]

The proposal that the animator should be introduced into the scene is not intended to mean that a proportion of Africa's population should be shut away in an oral ghetto. On the contrary, it is hoped that the success of the animator concept in opening up channels into and out of largely non-literate communities would open the way for more formal services that could build on improved communication and awareness. In this way, the animator's job would in many ways be a transitional one, providing a better basis for conventional library and information services, rather than a permanent substitute for such services. The animator could contribute much to the difficult process of introducing rudimentary library service, through the provision of simple reading rooms and book boxes by national library systems, along lines which we will discuss later. At the same time, by strengthening and emphasizing the role of oramedia, the animator could do much to ensure that traditional communication was not ignored even when communities enjoyed the full range of modern services.

Libraries and education

Africa is often presented as a continent where reading is an alien and unpopular activity. The colonial education system, inherited by Africa and expanded since independence, presented reading as something to be learned, rather than a means to enjoyment. The skill of reading is taught in a mechanical and inflexible way, and books are commonly associated with the hard grind of study, rather than the luxury of leisure. What is more, both the content of the books and the solitude required to read them conflict with traditional values, making them at once less comprehensible and less acceptable. Parents who cannot read themselves, and who are uneasy about what their children are learning, do not provide the necessary home support and encouragement, and the homes themselves are overcrowded, noisy and, after sunset, too dark for the printed word to be seen. Even many of Africa's educated elite are non-readers, content only to use the printed word to pass exams and acquire certificates, but once free from the tyranny of books, reluctant to read again.

The conclusion which most commentators tend to draw from all this is that Africa presents a hostile environment to library development and that only after such obstacles have been overcome, and the preconditions for a reading society have been set in place, will the library start to fulfil its true potential. This line of argument has consoled librarians who are anxious about the poor reaction of the community to the services they provide. Indeed, it has become such a standard formula that its recitation tends to blind those who adopt it to causes for optimism. Henry Chakava has pointed out that "Readership surveys conducted during the last five years in countries like Nigeria, Kenya, Benin, Ghana, and Uganda have shown that more and more people, especially the young, are reading for pleasure".[20]

As an example of such survey evidence, the Kenya National Academy for Advancement of Arts and Science's *Survey of reading habits and preferences*,[21] which was published in 1980, found 91 percent of children claiming to read for pleasure. The supporting information, such as the expressed preference for comics over story books, lends credibility to the findings. The children also expressed a stronger preference for stories with distant rather than local settings. This runs directly counter to the accepted wisdom that lack of local content is the main disincentive to reading among African children. This does not automatically absolve publishers, booksellers and library acquisitions sections from the obligation to foster books with local content, for no body of readers will be properly served if it cannot read good books dealing with familiar issues faced by recognizable characters in well-known settings. It does, however, go a long way towards removing the anxiety that exotic settings will not draw and retain readers. The success, in terms of sales, of recent works of locally-published fiction, in particular in Nigeria, Kenya, and Zimbabwe, provides ample evidence both that Africans do continue reading after their formal education and that they do not only read imported material. Moreover, their reading is not only for utilitarian purposes or achievement, as is so often claimed.

The total population of sub-Saharan Africa is about 450 million and is growing at an annual average rate of over 3 percent. The cumulative effect of this sort of growth in recent decades is that nearly half of the population is under the age of fifteen. The prospect of a population doubled in size and still containing a very high proportion of young people by the beginning of the twenty-first century is a very real one. The majority of these young people receive formal schooling and are gaining the basic skills of literacy, which their parents less commonly had available to them. The trend of population growth alone is reason to believe that a reading society is in process of emerging.

Service to young people

The future for Africa's libraries can be found in the one common
characteristic that this rapidly growing population possesses, that is,
its desperate thirst for education. Libraries have a responsibility to
make a contribution towards educating them. Africa's governments
have long recognized this by devoting extremely large percentages,
often as much as one third of their total expenditure, to education.
What governments and ministries of education seem less frequently to
accept, or even consider, is that book and library provision should
form an essential component of this investment. Nor, for that matter,
has the library profession recognized the significance of the information dimension in education. It is extremely unfortunate that Africa's
librarians have neglected this sector, where the potential demand for
library services is greatest, and the need arguably strongest. In this
they are following a precedent set often in the past in other continents
for public library service to children to be comparatively undervalued,
and school library service to be relegated to the last place on the scale of
priorities.

Such biases have a particularly unfortunate effect when transferred
to Africa. It is not uncommon to find a public library swarming with
school children but devoid of adult readers. The collection may boast
what appears to be an impressive stock of adult material, well
organized, inviting, and representative of the type of materials to be
found in most British branch libraries. Set alongside this will be the
children's section, comprising a few tattered and filthy books, hidden
away in some remote part of the library, uninviting, badly organized,
and clearly forming a marginal part of the librarian's concern. Even
where some semblance of a school library does exist, it is frequently
inadequately staffed, with an appallingly sparse collection, and is thus
marginal in terms of its impact on the teaching-learning process.
The majority of schools possess no library and no librarian, just a
few jealously-guarded books which are locked away from the prying
fingers of eager and clamorous children anxious to acquire fresh
knowledge.

The current debate on the future of libraries reflects only the barest
appreciation of the vital importance of service to Africa's young
people. The typical menu of story hours, play readings, film shows,
painting competitions, quizzes and talks is certainly in evidence, but
not frequently, and is rarely a priority of public library activity. Book
box schemes to remote rural areas, usually involving schools,

represent a typical response of library systems. As a beginning they are important, but the size of the collection and the frequency of its exchange are seldom sufficient to satisfy or nurture a demand for books and reading.

Cases of more responsive approaches can be found, but are extremely rare. For example, when in 1975 a user survey of three new branch libraries in Lusaka, Zambia, showed that 60 percent of users were children who did not attend school, the bulk of the funds for purchasing additional material for the libraries was directed towards their needs. Zimbabwe too has shown willingness to take a more positive approach to the needs of young readers. A Children's Literature Foundation has been set up to encourage Zimbabwean writing for children, and story sessions in the children's own languages have been organized by libraries. Small collections of books suitable for parents and children to read together have been distributed via the Association of Adult Literacy, and the intention is to make these as widely available as possible, even to the extent of lodging them in private houses if no formal library structure exists. A more typical situation, unfortunately, was that in Kenya in 1978, when a 75 percent cut in the Kenya National Library Service budget resulted in the cessation of all purchases of children's material. Even the excellent township libraries of Bulawayo, in Zimbabwe, have sometimes been forced by lack of sufficient books to withdraw the lending service to children. As recently as 1986 it was possible to find it stated that "Library service to children is a virgin area in Nigerian librarianship".[22]

It is not just the swiftly growing number of young people that calls for a more positive response to the library and information needs of children; there are also compelling arguments within Africa's educational system which call for a greater library involvement. To the casual observer, the education of its citizens since independence can be counted as one of Africa's success stories. From extremely inauspicious beginnings, when education was the preserve of a tiny minority, primary education is now no longer a dream for most children, the doors of secondary schools are opening to a growing majority, and increasing opportunities for tertiary level education and training are becoming available. Yet education in Africa is in deep crisis, a crisis of similar proportions to that in which librarianship finds itself, but one of far greater consequence.

From colonial times up until the present day the general character of education in Africa has been identified as a system whose purpose is examination rather than education. The whole focus of attention is on the final examination, which can only be passed by strictly following the prescribed curriculum, which must be taught in the prescribed way, usually following a single prescribed textbook. Rote learning is the norm, with good books and good teachers generally being in short supply. A large number of the primary level workforce are ill-prepared and ill-equipped to teach effectively, the secondary work-force is overstretched and undermotivated, while the university sector is disenchanted, lacking the essential research resources upon which good university-level teaching depends. As a result, children and students are *taught*, rather than being encouraged to *learn*, and what is worse, they are all taught the same facts, at the same time and in the same way, regardless of their abilities.[23]

The 'book famine' or 'book hunger' which we have referred to before does not merely mean an absence of libraries in schools, but also a dire shortage of textbooks. Pupils share books that were designed to be studied individually, books are passed on from year to year, getting more and more tattered with each new group of users, and parents who can ill afford it are required to contribute money for the purchase of the necessary books that the state cannot provide. What exists is an educational system which does not provide the type of environment in which innovation and creative ideas can flourish. Yet the crisis in education is even more serious than this.

The faith in education as a means for both the salvation of the individual and the nation, which inspired the leaders of African independence and convinced them to invest a considerable financial outlay, has been severely tested in recent years. The modern employment sector, which witnessed a boom after independence, has for a decade or more stagnated and declined, with insufficient jobs being created to satisfy the aspirations of an increasingly educated workforce. Unemployment began to emerge among primary school leavers in the 1960s, among secondary school leavers in the 1970s, and has begun to affect university graduates. Although shortage of suitably qualified personnel is still described as one of Africa's more persistent problems, the educational system's achievements have generally not been in the direction of providing those personnel, but instead in producing a better qualified cadre of the unemployed.

This has led to a serious crisis of confidence in education, which in the past has generally been regarded as a vital component of successful economic performance. Although some writers still reaffirm the "profound beneficial implications of education in development,"[24] there is no longer unanimity on this. The counter view is that education cannot simply be treated as a contributor to economic success, but may, on the contrary, be a luxury to be enjoyed when that economic success has been achieved. As one writer puts it, "Independence raised the expectations of the ordinary man in Africa. He asked for the good things of life which had been promised before independence. One of these good things was education".[25] Unfortunately that education has not necessarily resulted in jobs, and the benefits accruing from spending many years in the classroom are becoming increasingly illusory. This has led to the development of a revisionist, indeed, some may claim heretical view, that attempts to remove education almost completely from the development agenda. Such views were articulated in the early 1970s by economists who questioned the entire premise that education in abundance beyond literacy is an unmitigated social good and an engine for development. They argued that, on the contrary, education was capable of being an investment in idle human resources. An understanding of how such an argument has evolved is essential because of its implications for library service.

Whilst in the 1950s and 1960s there was a great need for educated personnel, by the end of the 1960s, the argument runs, this was not matched by a real increase in new jobs. This was not noticed immediately because the demand for workers generated by localization and the ambitious projects of new governments was not seen as a temporary phase, but rather as a normal condition. But gradually it began to emerge that education and employment creation were not marching properly in step. Suggestions as to why this happened, apart from the general economic climate, include the import of labour-saving technology; the comparatively high wages being paid to modern sector employees, which forced employers to limit staffing levels; the continuing dependence on expatriate staff and, paradoxically, the success, over the last three decades, in opening up educational opportunities. The question as to whether Africa is over-investing in education beyond literacy is now part of the debate. The implications of this line of argument are as catastrophic for libraries as they are for education. Yet the library profession has so far failed to engage in the dialogue, and if the literature of librarianship in Africa is any guideline, has completely failed to appreciate that such a dialogue is even taking place.

As yet the argument has not been satisfactorily resolved, although there is some evidence to support a reassertion of the more optimistic view of education.[26] The World Bank, for instance, which prefers its involvement to be confined to areas where a quantifiable outcome can be guaranteed, generally seems to accept the view that countries which invest heavily in schooling have measurable advantages over those that do not. Some countries which have substantially improved their ranking in economic indicators in recent years—Togo and the Congo for instance—have a correspondingly strong commitment to educational investment while others, such as Niger, Burkina Faso, Uganda and Somalia, which have a poor or declining record of schooling, have not improved economically in a comparable way. What the figures seem to show is that where education, particularly primary education, is more readily available there tend to be higher levels of personal income and associated improvements in nutrition and health. The sequence of causation is open to question, and it would be easy to argue that the improvements do not arise from the benefits of education, but at least this line of argument is some relief from the pessimism about education that has prevailed recently.

Gloomy views of education may seem to suggest that the prospects for library services to education are gloomy too. In practice the opposite could be true: the very crises in which education is currently enveloped may enable library and information work to establish a better future for itself. The crisis has provoked thinking about new and more appropriate educational models for the continent. The various new approaches which are emerging have much in common with each other. The guiding principle behind them has been described as 'pedagogical decentralization'[27], which amounts to a move away from centralized curricula towards learning that is better matched to the needs of the individual and the community. This has led to a different view of formal schooling in Africa, which suggests that—'Formal schooling is essentially complementary in nature to less formal systems that impart vocational skills and the weaknesses of many earlier educational strategies lay in their disregard of the existence of highly efficient informal educational structures. Perhaps formal schooling largely through the provision of literacy, numeracy, and general education generates a basic 'ability to learn' that is vital in the innovatory development process''.[28] Less formal schooling and emphasis on existing informal structures present good opportunities for the new librarianship we are advocating.

The systems being referred to include 'education with production'. This is probably best known through the work of Patrick van Rensberg in Botswana, and it reasserts the values of traditional education by imparting useful skills through practical experience, alongside more conventional schooling.[29] Other new curricula which are broadly conceived and more adaptive to Africa's educational needs are constantly being developed, tested, and revised. All these approaches start from a perception of the needs of citizens in society as it presently is and as it might be in the immediate future. Moreover, all emphasize an enhanced interaction between the teacher and the taught, and lay particular stress on the importance of the teaching and learning materials that are part of that process. Yet the implications for libraries, although seemingly quite obvious, have not been taken up by Africa's librarians. Their response has seldom gone beyond a half-hearted plea for governments to provide more school libraries.

African librarians themselves are still only half convinced of the importance of librarianship for young people, and they do not in general place a very high value on school libraries. Despite many years of effort throughout the world to promote a positive view of librarianship for young people, it is still quite common to hear senior librarians make disparaging remarks about children's literature or those who think that it is important. School libraries are particularly likely to be neglected or ignored whilst this mentality persists, for their librarians work largely alone and have difficulty in finding means to present a collective case for their specialization. Teachers, as distinct from educational theorists, are even harder to convince of the value of libraries. Too many of them are content to persist with the rigid and sterile teaching methods which they themselves experienced as children. Such attitudes contribute to a very unfavourable environment for the improvement of school libraries and the practice of school librarianship.

For this situation to be improved, the education of librarians needs to place a much stronger emphasis on the rationale for school libraries and the techniques of school librarianship. African library schools can make a major contribution by striving to ensure that their graduates meet these requirements. There is also the need for those responsible for library services in their countries to promote the inclusion of a more positive approach towards school libraries in the courses provided by institutions of teacher training. When both librarians and teachers are more firmly convinced of the case for libraries in schools there will be scope for a better case to be made to ministries of education than is done at present. This is no easy programme but it is a vital one if, as we feel is essential, school libraries are to be an effective part of a new approach to librarianship in Africa.

Libraries and literacy programmes

The case for services to support basic literacy programmes has been made more effectively than the case for school libraries. Generally speaking, those who have made the case have been adult educators rather than librarians, but increasing numbers of librarians are accepting the significance of this form of service. This is important because the scope for work in conjunction with literacy programmes is immense. Despite the enormous advances that Africa has achieved since independence in making formal education available to a growing proportion of the continent's population, the skills of reading and writing are, for many still an extremely fragile acquisition. This includes even those who have gone through the formal school system at primary and secondary levels. Precise estimates of the numbers who are literate are difficult to obtain. Those that are available are unreliable, and mask extreme variations between town and village, between different generations, and between different geographical regions. Even a simple definition of what constitutes literacy can rarely be agreed. It is hardly surprising in such circumstances that the only constant feature of Africa's literacy statistics are their wild variations, and their unpredictable fluctuations. It is therefore to the accounts of what is actually happening within the continent to improve and extend literacy that we must turn to for a treatment of this topic.

Detailed description of the adult literacy programme in Ethiopia is available,[30] and although war and famine in that country make it in some ways an unsuitable choice of example, what is described does give helpful insights into the typical difficulties involved in attempting to provide reading and writing skills to an entire population, almost overnight. At the time of the revolution in 1974 which saw the overthrow of the Emperor Haile Selassie, only 1.38 million adults (defined as the 10–45 age group) in urban areas, and 1.05 million adults in rural areas, were estimated to be literate. This was from a total population then in excess of 20 million, and in a country almost unique in Africa for its ancient literary culture. The National Literacy Campaign, launched in 1979, set out with the aim of providing permanent literacy for every Ethiopian. The campaign was organized over a number of twelve-month periods, each consisting of two distinct 'rounds'. The first round was referred to as the 'attack' round, when literacy classes were offered to everyone in the community over the age of eight years. This was followed by a 'mop up' round, in which those who failed the test at the end of the first round could obtain remedial tuition and the previously successful students receive back-up attention. Fourteen such rounds had been completed in 1986, with each attack round catering for 1 to 1.5 million people, and the mop-up rounds for 0.5 million.

The actual success of this campaign is hard to judge, the numbers involved being so enormous, and the vocabulary used to describe it conveying more the tone of a military exercise than a programme to nurture and develop the refined tastes usually associated with literature and reading. Nevertheless the claim is that 13.5 million people, over 60 percent of the current population, are now literate, as opposed to only 7 percent before the revolution. The aim is to make the entire population literate by the end of the literacy campaign in 1991. The fact that even the richest developed countries now accept that a small but significant percentage of their population is not, for various reasons, fully literate, has not impinged upon those leading the campaign in Ethiopia. Leaving this aside, the hopes and aspirations of this campaign are typical of this type of programme, with the primary objective being to have ''an impact on productivity and organisational capacity which will contribute to a rise in GDP per capita and a higher degree of self reliance''.[31]

Already the Ethiopian campaign has had to adjust to the realization that, as nearly 40 percent of literacy course participants fail to gain their certificate, and require one or more subsequent courses, the campaign must inevitably continue well beyond 1991. In addition, a post-literacy phase has had to be introduced, linked to the community education services which are being developed in parallel with the literacy campaign. Post-literacy programmes include:

a. the establishment of community reading rooms (of which it is claimed over 7,000 have been designated) with the premises provided by the community and the publications by the campaign organization;
b. the development of a network of community skill training centres (with a planned 588 to be set up in the first phase);
c. the establishment of a network of regional radio stations for educational programmes;
d. a four-page literacy bulletin which the Campaign Co-ordinating Committee already distributes in the Amharic, Oromo, and Tigraian languages and intends to publish in other vernaculars;
e. the encouragement of Basic Education Centres in rural settlements to provide an organizational framework for the application of literacy skills to development needs;
f. the creation of a network of Awraja (District) Pedagogical Centres to

bring together educational personnel, representatives of popular associations, and the general public for the encouragement of community involvement in all types of educational institutions and programmes.

More directly linked to the literacy campaign is the preparation of reading materials in such areas as agricultural skills, health and nutrition, child care, and the skills of local traditional industry. Enthusiastic take-up of literacy courses in communities of many different kinds is often followed by a swift tailing-off of interest when practical advantages from the hard-earned skills are not obvious. Literacy needs to be obviously worth the trouble it takes to acquire, and publishing materials on topics of everyday importance seems the most direct way of confirming this. Nevertheless, the sheer volume of material needed in the fifteen languages of the Ethiopian literacy campaign is daunting. Millions of copies would be required to supply the 1,000 publications envisaged as a norm in each of the envisaged 30,000 village reading rooms. An obvious problem is the enormous strain on financial resources created by the need to import most of the paper required. There are, however, a multitude of other rather more complex problems associated with a programme of this type. These can be explored by considering what has taken place in Tanzania, a country with considerable experience of publishing to support literacy work.

Tanzania launched its National Literacy Campaign as long ago as 1970 and immediately recognized the need for reading materials appropriate to the needs of new literates, with rural newspapers in Swahili forming a major part of the proposed answer to the problem.[32] Unesco and the Norwegian Agency for Development (NORAD) provided the initial funding in 1974 to produce a rural paper for the Lake Zone, *Elimu Haina Mwisho* (Education has no end). It was launched with an initial print run of 25,000 copies, and because of its early success and ready acceptance by the communities it served, six other rural newspapers on a similar plan were eventually launched in the Eastern, Southern, Southern Highland, Central, and Western Zones. A four-page newspaper containing both information and entertainment is now provided for very large numbers of the Tanzanian rural population. The format is standard to all the papers, with page one covering national news, page two local news; page three is a miscellany including letters, and page four is a practical page with material on topics such as 'How to grow better cotton' or 'How to make a wheelbarrow'. Circulation of *Elimu Haina Mwisho* has now been built up to 100,000 and the other papers each have a print run of around 50,000 copies. The process of achieving this has not, however, been a simple one; both production and distribution have involved considerable difficulties.

The plan for each newspaper is that it will be wholly produced in its own zone. At present this can be achieved at least as far as the stage at which the copy is pasted up into the sheets which will go into the printing process. To achieve this, offices for each newspaper have had to be established. The finance for this has been the responsibility of the donor agencies, which have also undertaken to provide the basic equipment, train staff, and cover printing costs. In the first place the offices have been temporary arrangements while more permanent premises were developed. The team at each office consists of an editor assisted by six people—a journalist/assistant editor, photolithographer, typist-compositor, messenger, watchman and driver. In addition each paper has its own news-gathering network through officers at the regional education headquarters and in the districts and at ward level through education co-ordinators.

The link with the education system is further emphasized through the advisory boards which all the newspapers have. The membership includes regional education officers and adult education co-ordinators. They are chaired by a regional development director and have the newspaper editor as secretary. Membership also includes a representative from the Tanzanian News Agency (SHIHATA), and regional agriculture and health officers. To confirm this link even more strongly, the two editorial members of the newspaper staff are not journalists by profession, but are recruited from education, in particular from among educationists with experience in adult education and literacy programmes at the local level. Recruitment from one profession, that of education, to another, journalism, has not been problem-free. Retraining has been an important element, with the editors attending journalism courses within Tanzania in addition to practical attachments to the pioneer rural newspaper office of *Elimu Haina Mwisho*. Despite the difficulties caused by the merging of two distinct professions, the original objective, that the newspapers should retain a direct link with the adult education and literacy function, has not been abandoned.

There are, however, still more difficulties. The logic of having the offices for the rural newspapers based in the communities they are intended to serve also indicates that the production process should be there too. Integration of news gathering, editing and production is too sensible an arrangement to require justification, but achieving it has proved exceedingly difficult. Although the parent newspaper, *Elimu Haina Mwisho*, now has its own production equipment, at the beginning much of the press work had to be contracted out. This is still the case with all the other newspapers, which have no alternative but to resort to outside printers who produce the newspapers under contract. This involves all the problems which seem to arise when control of one of the vital elements in such a scheme is lost. The printers' priorities seldom seem to be the same as those of the editors; they do not always have the technical facilities to produce the papers in the way the editor wants; and outside contracting tends to mean additional costs. The installation of full production facilities at all the rural newspaper offices is a priority, not only to solve the problems of contracting out, but also to commence the production of other literacy support materials.

Distribution is the final key element and source of difficulties for the rural newspapers. Even if the editorial and production processes have gone smoothly there is still the problem of getting the newspaper out to its readers each month. From the regional headquarters the papers are sent by four-wheel drive vehicle to the districts, from where they are further redistributed to individual readers via adult education field staff at ward level, using book bags fitted to bicycles. In rural Africa this represents an extremely fragile and vulnerable chain of delivery, which often results in newspapers not reaching their readers.

Without doubt literacy campaigns in both Ethiopia and Tanzania are faced with difficulties, but too great an emphasis on their problems would not be fair. The Ethiopian campaign by virtue of its sheer scale, and the Tanzanian one in terms of its important contribution to the post-literacy phase, provide valuable lessons for others involved in the same work. So far we have mentioned little of the role of formal library services in relation to literacy campaigns in Africa. The reason is that they are doing only a little as yet, although there are some promising indications from Africa's librarians of a shift in their attention towards this direction.

Librarians are deeply committed to books and to the people who possess the skills to read them. To many in the library profession, imagining users who can barely read or write in the book-dominated environment of the library is quite an alien concept. So far, Africa's public librarians do not seem to have incorporated this category of potential user into their library strategy. This is hardly surprising since the public libraries of North America, Britain, and much of Europe, on which African public libraries were modelled, were designed in response to the needs of societies which were sometimes talked of as if they were completely literate and were, indeed, substantially so. The subsequent history of public libraries; the types of service they have provided, the training of their staff, the design of buildings, the development and organization of collections, have, despite the perception of a few librarians that there was work to be done in supporting new literates, all followed from this implicit assumption. African systems based on this model have absorbed the basic assumption along with its visible consequences.

There is, nevertheless, some experience of the use of a less formal type of reading institution stretching back many years in Nigeria, where village reading rooms were set up by the British colonial administration to publicize the Allied war effort during the Second World War. They originally contained radios, newspapers, maps, pamphlets, and a few books. They were allowed to decline and disappear after the war, although some efforts were made to revive them during the 1950s. To librarians they were generally a source of annoyance, despite evidence that they had been useful in relation to literacy programmes. The usual library response to them was summed up by a Nigerian librarian who said that "their administration made it impossible for us to convert them to libraries. The functions they were created to serve are in direct conflict with our ideas of a public library service".[33]

In other parts of the continent the reading room idea has been revived and reconstituted in a modern equivalent, explicitly in connection with literacy programmes. Indeed, an important point about such schemes is that they do arise much more from the activities of adult education organizations than from library services. To librarians the idea seems less like an innovation and more like a retreat from full library provision to an inferior level of service. We do not believe that the idea has to be seen in this way. Whilst existing resources patently do not permit full library service to be delivered to more than a small number of communities, there is a strong case for providing the much less expensive reading rooms to a much larger number of communities. This can ensure both a more effective and a fairer distribution of available resources. Even more important is the fact that the reading room concept is very appropriate to the present needs of many communities.

Reading institutions, which respond directly to African circumstances, may often need to be much simpler than their northern counterparts. Literacy programmes, for instance, create certain straightforward needs. One is for a quiet place, away from the bustle of family life, where it is possible to concentrate on reading. The very brief period of fading light which is all that may be available to the reader after a full day of work in the fields, the factory, or domestic service, dictates that this place must have artificial light. The reading room concept is a simple response to these needs, providing unpretentious facilities, with a few tables, chairs, and some simple reading material of an appropriate kind, and wherever possible some means of artificial light. Such rooms are sometimes referred to as village libraries, but in essence they are a much more basic type of facility. Mention of the use of village reading rooms has already been made in relation to Ethiopia, but the systems that are already in use in Tanzania and Botswana show what the generalizations actually mean.

There are over 3,000 village libraries in Tanzania,[34] with about 400 titles available in each. They are under the supervision of the local adult education co-ordinators, part of whose job it is to encourage the local authorities to provide standardized buildings. At present they are often to be found in a variety of premises, such as primary schools, clinics, court houses, the offices of co-operatives, and even private houses. Shelving, catalogue drawers, date stamps, and the usual paraphernalia associated with libraries are absent. What the reading rooms do have is readers.

The difficulty of actually establishing this type of system at village level, as opposed to conceptualizing it from the desk of a ministry building in the capital, can be seen from recent experience in Botswana,[35] where such a system is in its infancy. Government commitment to the initial provision of over 300 reading rooms by the Department of Non-Formal Education in small village communities throughout the country was achieved with comparative ease. The translation of this approval into effective practice is where the difficulties occurred. A pilot project in the Kgatleng District was tried first. Local institutions gave some early encouragement by agreeing to provide premises, but changes of mind on the part of Village Development Committees or Land Board officials led to the eventual use of a primary school, and a Botswana National Library Service branch library as the first sites. Schools, as one of the most widely distributed public facilities, are frequently hosts to reading rooms, although their function in educating children may incline some adult new literates, sensitive of their status, to avoid them.

The use of a National Library Service branch may seem slightly ironical, since reading rooms are essentially intended to be alternative or complementary to libraries. It is to the credit of the National Library Service's staff that co-operation has been offered, even though the initiative for the scheme was not theirs and it might easily be perceived as rivalling their functions. Encouragingly, extension of the Botswana National Library Service's book box scheme, at present provided for schools, has been discussed as a means of providing reading rooms with small collections of reading material that can be changed at regular intervals. For library systems not to be involved with the reading rooms at all would surely be very unfortunate. It is to library systems that communities must look eventually for upgrading of service when they outgrow the facilities that a reading room can provide. The kind of co-operation that seems to be emerging in Botswana is very much needed, both in the short term and for this eventual upgrading, but the beginnings are very tentative.

No doubt at the early stages there were difficulties in setting up reading rooms in Tanzania and cooperation with the National Library Service has probably been no more straightforward than in Botswana. Currently, the reading rooms are staffed by someone who is referred to as a 'village librarian'. This village librarian is selected from the village community, with no more than a primary level standard of education. The same person often also performs the functions of a literacy group tutor. In return for the payment of an honorarium equal to one eighth of the national minimum wage, the village librarian is expected to open the reading room and supervise its use, as well as organizing discussion groups around what is currently being read. Their training is a one-month course at a Folk Development College, alongside people taking similar courses on health, agriculture, or building. The courses are said to suffer from a dearth of instructional material in Swahili and insufficient follow-up has also been seen as a limitation but, at the very least, they make a contribution by reinforcing the village librarians' motivation and morale.

The development of village reading rooms in Tanzania is clearly not problem-free. Irregular arrival of the honorarium, imprecise lines of responsibility, lack of helpful contact with the central administration, all tend to act as a disincentive to the village librarian to become a committed proselytizer of the reading room concept. Shortage of reading materials is an even worse obstacle. The bulk of the stock is supposed to be in Swahili, the language in which people learn to read. Despite this intention, an increasing proportion now tends to be the English language product of foreign-owned commercial publishers. No reliable way seems to have been found, in Tanzania or elsewhere, to produce enough material in the people's mother tongues to meet the need. Whether this is a problem of writers or of publishers, little seems to have been achieved in coping with it. Its consequence is to limit the number of publications which are comprehensible to new literates. This means that the most enthusiastic readers can easily exhaust all the material made available to them and lose interest in visiting the reading room.

Such problems have to be faced, but they do not destroy the validity of the reading room concept. The reading room, given some improved administrative support and a large enough supply of suitable reading material, is capable of providing for the immediate needs of new readers. When the readers are much more numerous and their demand for reading material and information is sufficiently intense and varied, there is scope for genuine expansion of public library systems to meet their requirements. Until then, concentration on the reading room and the school library should form the core of a programme for library work. Although this places the emphasis very much on involvement with education, it clearly omits any proposal for higher education. This is the next problem that we will deal with, treating it alongside service to specialists of all types.

Service to the committed information user

Two kinds of committed information user are now sufficiently numerous and important as to require institutions and services devoted to their needs. They are first, those involved in higher education, whether they are students, teachers or researchers, and secondly, specialists involved in administration and non-academic research. In the case of these two groups we are inevitably talking about provision of libraries on a conventional plan.

Academic libraries are inevitably expensive to provide. Wherever they are in the world, they need to stock large quantities of costly publications, many of them imported, and they are likely to require elaborate bibliographic and related services in support. Their staff must necessarily be highly trained. Because academic libraries are so costly, it is arguable that they are the type of library which suffers most damagingly from the poverty of African countries. A recent examination of the collections of academic libraries in Nigeria showed that, before 1979, 80 percent of total collections consisted of imported

material (with the figure for journals taken alone reaching 90 percent).[36] Import restrictions and exchange controls have subsequently
reduced imports virtually to nothing, and collections are much dimin-
ished in size and scope. To some extent the case of Nigeria is an
unhelpful example, because its considerable wealth in the 1970s distorted the position. Academic libraries were able to import materials
in a way that those of other countries have never been able to contemplate. The ideal of the university library as a very large teaching and
research resource was the guiding principle, and in a few cases this led
to quite profligate expenditure. The crisis of Nigerian academic
libraries in the 1980s merely brought them into a position comparable
with that of their fellows in other African countries.

Financial crisis has been alleviated to a very limited extent by tactics
such as buying from local suppliers whenever possible, developing
exchange programmes, the use of Unesco coupons, and resource
sharing schemes. More rigorous management of stock, to ensure that
what is bought and kept on the shelves is really needed and will be
used, is to some extent a positive consequence of the difficulties.
Moves to stimulate local academic publishing, fraught with difficulties though they may be, are also very positive. In the end, however, a strict realism over the role that the academic library can hope to
play in the immediate future is essential. This means that the research
library, accumulating materials speculatively on the grounds that
future researchers may value them, is an unrealistic concept. University libraries have to accept a role much more directly tied to teaching.
Research collecting is better handled at this stage by specialized institutes which collect in very specific and well-defined fields. These may
be administered by the university itself in some cases, but they may
also be the special libraries which we will discuss shortly.

Despite these comments, if one sector of library and information
work can be identified to which it is most appropriate to direct the
assistance of aid agencies, then that sector is academic libraries. The
form such aid might take is of considerable importance. Unsystematic
donations of books and other materials by aid and charitable agencies,
as discussed earlier, are of mixed value. More interestingly, there has
been some discussion of concepts such as 'consolidation of information' to improve the effectiveness of the assistance that can be provided.[37] This concept involves some agency evaluating and
condensing information materials (books, reports, serials or whatever) for distribution to institutions serving specific user groups.
Condensing means selecting, summarizing and, possibly, physically

reducing material in size by the use of forms such as microfiche or CD-ROM. The groups served might be any group of specialists such as medical students or civil engineers, and the institutions involved would frequently be academic libraries.

Special libraries and information services are the sector of librarianship which already shows the most positive signs of vitality in many parts of the continent. The special library, whether it be in a government department or a research institute, is often small and may be able to function without too much imported literature. It is comparatively easy for some agency to begin to accumulate a few publications and files, subscribe to some journals or information services, and find that it has begun to provide a special library facility without realizing that anything of the kind was happening. The formalization of a budget for such service and the employment of suitably trained personnel is a later and sometimes rather more difficult stage. One can identify many cases of this process of institutions responding naturally to demand for information, but it seems to have happened more in some sectors than others.

Some of the very first special libraries in Africa were those of national geological surveys. As long ago as 1967 an account of more than twenty of these was published.[38] Few had professional librarians, but several had qualified geologists as information officers. Their collections had few books, but many reprints, pamphlets, maps, microforms and photographs. These libraries were originally a response to colonial perceptions of the importance of the mineral wealth of African countries, but subsequently they have become a means by which independent nations seek to assemble the information they need to cope with the prospecting activities of multinational companies. The vast financial resources of these companies enable them to use modern techniques like remote sensing to detect the significant variations of the earth's surface which might indicate the presence of valuable mineral resources. Faced with the ability of organizations from outside the nation's boundaries to accumulate information of the most crucial commercial and strategic importance, the state has to ensure that its ability to insist on the deposit of full prospecting documentation is as effective as possible. Well run geological survey libraries and records centres are a means to this end.

Agriculture is nowadays the most common subject area for the provision of special libraries. Of the more than twenty government research institutes in Nigeria, the majority are concerned with agriculture.[39] Despite the fact that a survey of their libraries in 1983 suggested that all of these were inadequately funded and had serious deficiencies in their buildings, collections and services,[40] their very existence is significant. These libraries are not visited by farmers to any significant extent[41] but they are definitely an essential resource for the researcher, and potentially important for those who prepare information materials for farmers, or the equivalent ultimate target group in other disciplines. At present, the circulars and pamphlets prepared for distribution to farmers are not especially effective, and the experience is cited of those who have "bought kitchen salt, soda or curry powder usually sold by the spoon in the groceries and markets in the townships and villages and found copies of the publications used as wrapping".[42]

Library services certainly do not perform to their full potential as repackagers of information for use by agents like agricultural extension workers. If the role of such agents (preferably in the guise of the information animator as we have earlier suggested) is to take on the significance of which it is capable, then information institutions must do more to make this possible. This means that they must take up the task of repackaging with much more enthusiasm than at present. The difficulty is that the tasks are unfamiliar. As one writer put it, "Some libraries and information centres in less developed countries found themselves in the position of writers, rewriters, popularisers and publishers of literature—a role for which they are not well suited".[43]

There is a certain amount of published information on experimentation with repackaging. This suggests interesting lessons, such as the strong and encouraging possibility that methods enlisting traditional media, rather than modern mass media, are not only more effective but also cheaper. There is, however, by no means enough of this experimentation in relation to the importance of the subject. What is even less available is evaluation of this experimentation. Diana Rosenberg, in calling for more evaluation, poses questions on topics such as the long-term success of projects, and the extent to which information provided to one group has been subsequently transferred in some form to other groups.[44] There is obviously a considerable research programme arising from repackaging, and it provides a more realistic focus for the work of students taking higher degrees in library and information studies than some of those at present chosen.

As for the materials collected by special libraries, these are more frequently grey literature rather than the output of conventional publishing houses. Such material may not always be preferred by users, but analysis of the citations in a number of African research theses in agriculture suggested that already 14 percent of the material used was grey literature, mainly consisting of technical reports and conference proceedings.[45] As we have suggested earlier, this material is hard to acquire, but it has the advantage of frequently being free (in the sense of not having to be paid for directly), and not calling for great resources of foreign currency. A special library with a well-organized acquisitions programme can realistically hope to build good collections of grey literature by hard work rather than the expenditure of large sums of money. This is not true of conventional publications, and ways of alleviating this problem are naturally sought. One way which is frequently offered is the adoption of co-operative and interlending schemes. Boadi, however, points out that "Cooperative acquisition schemes have been tried with disappointing results and interlending programmes have in most cases proved equally unsuccessful".[46]

The onus still remains firmly on the individual library or information office to provide the maximum it can, without hoping for too much from any other agency. Observation suggests that this is a challenge the special library copes with well. The sector needs help, but not building from ground level, or rebuilding from a shaky existing structure as is the case in other sectors.

Conclusion

What we have already said about existing library service in Africa quite clearly points to the need for new types of library and new types of librarian who can provide a more direct challenge to Africa's information problems. Creating a library model that is less formal, less book-oriented, more locally rooted, and more precisely targeted at Africa's real and potential information users, is the challenge now confronting Africa's librarians. The new paradigm of library service that does emerge from this challenge must be firmly based on the needs and characteristics of the ordinary citizens, in particular the citizens of tomorrow.

The base line for this realignment must be the traditional oral culture. Advocating the exploitation of these media may seem to be clutching at straws, but in fact there is the strongest case for drawing into the mainstream of modern life elements that have been unjustly neglected. There is much essential historical, environmental, spiritual, agricultural, scientific, and medical knowledge in the corpus of tradition, that must be better used. The use of sound- and video-recording equipment can partly answer some of the need for the preservation and exploitation of this tradition, but it can do little more than freeze these cultural products for posterity. A much more radical *rapprochement* between modern and traditional information systems, in which oral exchange and the written word complement each other, is the ideal to be aimed for. In this way information from outside the community could be delivered in traditional ways, but more importantly the resources of tradition can be harnessed and given a more pronounced focus for dissemination and use.

We are well aware that any such shift in emphasis will leave gaps in the conventional version of library and information provision. The national library as one of the essential symbols of national pride, alongside the national stadium and the international airport, for the moment has an insignificant role to play in this vision. The national library we see as a collecting and bibliographic organization concentrating on locally-produced materials. We see it as a reactive and flexible co-ordinating agency, rather than the impressive hub of an elaborately-constructed wheel. Expensive and time-consuming emphasis on formalizing national and regional networks, we see as premature. Over-elaboration in cataloguing and bibliographic work we see as inappropriate, preferring simple and timely solutions to problems of this kind. Electronic services for bibliographic information we see as being necessary in academic and research institutions, but otherwise of low priority in the general scheme of things.

Certainly the conventional public library, based on the European and North American model, is inappropriate, and (despite the rhetoric deployed in its support) insufficiently democratic to have priority in the current state of library and information work in Africa. The elaboration of buildings, equipment and furnishings we feel is unnecessary. Over-training of personnel, the too ready use of educational facilities outside the African continent, as well as the mimicking of European and North American curricula by African library schools, we would like to see discouraged. The gaps that are left when this new library model emerges are obviously regrettable, but we feel that until the base of library and information work in Africa is sounder and better established, some of the practices normally associated with librarianship will have to be postponed.

The ideas for priorities which we have suggested are in the first place based on an empirical approach—identifying needs and the available resources to meet those needs. They also accord with the general principle that Africa's future needs to be taken more firmly into the hands of Africans. A true Africanization means the adoption of policies of disengagement from the relationships of dependence with the northern industrial economies, and the assertion of self-reliance as the principle national goal. Without self-reliance it is likely that even the populations of those countries which do achieve real and substantial economic growth will obtain few of the benefits that should accrue from that growth. Self-reliant nations would not be aiming for some kind of complete economic and political separation from the rest of the world, but rather for the opportunity to control their own destinies, to seek solutions appropriate to their needs, and to be able to contemplate the eventual enjoyment of the fruits of these policies, themselves.

The struggle to establish self-reliance in information and communications has its public and hotly-debated aspect, namely, that which concerns journalism and the media. Accusations of censorship and intolerable restraints on the freedom of information have been hurled at those who advocate a more balanced flow of information between nations. Often attacked by the industrialized countries as being illiberal and even totalitarian, the quest by Africa's governments through the news media to exercise a firmer control of the flows of information in and out of the country is central to the argument for a new direction in library and information work. At present Africa is an importer of information materials and methods, and an exporter of raw data and news material. The information content is then repackaged and exported back to Africa, providing Africans with a provocatively ill-balanced picture of their lives. Their understanding of the world is formed by the knowledge that is made available from the industrialized countries, and their ability to interpret this is conditioned by the media through which this information is filtered. The world outside Africa does not know Africa in Africa's own terms.

The quieter part of the struggle concerns the less publicly-noticed library and information sector. Though little fuss is made about them, it is not unreasonable to claim that the publications and other information resources conventionally found in libraries have more long-term significance than what is written in newspapers or transmitted over the air. We do not claim to have produced a blueprint for a new library model, as that will have to emerge from the new generation of Africa's library and information workers themselves. What we hope we have achieved is to have encouraged the debate, and prompted the deliberations in the direction of producing a library model in which self reliance will be the principal cornerstone.

References

1. Ndiaye, R. Oral culture and libraries. *IFLA Journal*, 14, 1988. 40–46.
2. Aiyepeku, W.O. Information utilisation by policy makers in Nigeria. *Journal of Information Science*, 4, 1982. 203–211.
3. For example, Amaratunga, C. *and* Shute, J. Extension and adult learning in a Ghanaian community. *Canadian Journal of African Studies* 16, 1982. 549–6.
4. Kibirigi, H.M. Libraries and illiteracy in developing countries: a critical assessment. *Libri*, 27, 1977. 54–67. p 55.
5. Enahoro, P. When the men died. *Africa Now*, 47, 1985. 5.
6. Ugboajah, F.O. Oramedia in Africa. *In*: Ugboajah, F.O. *ed. Mass communication, culture and society in West Africa*. London, Hans Zell, 1985. 165–176.
7. Lewycky, D. *Tapestry—report from Odi Weavers*. Gaborone, National Institute of Research, 1977.
8. Byram, M.L. Odi Weavers: material culture, workers organization, and nonformal education in Botswana. *In*: Kidd, R. *and* Colletta, N. *eds. Tradition for development: indigenous structures and folk media in non-formal education*. Bonn, DSE, 1980. 207–244. p 230.
9. Adimorah, E.N.O. Information and documentation for integrated rural development in Africa. *Quarterly Bulletin of the International Association of Agricultural Librarians and Documentalists*, 29, 1984. 21–28. p 25.
10. Oyeoku, K.K. Publishing in Africa: breaking the development barrier. *In*: Oluwasanmi, E., McLean, E. *and* Zell, H. *eds. Publishing in Africa in the seventies*. Ife, University of Ife Press, 1975. p 280.
11. Rahnema, M. The sound library, a simple but revolutionary tool for development. *Unesco Journal of Information Science, Librarianship and Archives Administration*, 4, 1982. 151–158. pp 156–157.
12. Hall, B. *and* Freyh, B. Foreword. *In*: Kidd, R. *and* Colletta, N. *eds. Tradition for development: indigenous structures and folk media in non-formal education*. Bonn, DSE, 1980. 4–6.
13. Ugboajah, F.O. *op. cit.* p 172.
14. Durrani, S. Rural information in Kenya. *Information Development*, 1, 1985. 149–157.
15. Aboyade, B.O. *The Provision of Information for Rural Development*. Ibadan, Fountain Publications, 1987. pp 57–68.
16. Roling, N. Knowledge brokerage for increasing the relevance of agricultural research to African smallholders. *Rural Africana*, 27, 1975. 113–119.
17. Boafo, S. Utilising development communication strategies in African societies: a critical perspective. *Gazette. International Journal for Mass Communication*, 35, 1985. 83–92.
18. Fiofori, D. Traditional media and modern messages: a Nigerian study. *Rural Africana*, 27, 1975. 43–52.

19. Amaratunga, C, and Shute, J. *op. cit.* p 564.

20. Chakava, H. Reading in Africa—some obstacles. *IFLA Journal*, 10, 1984. p 351.

21. Kenya National Academy for Advancement of Arts and Sciences. *A survey of reading habits and preferences among Nairobi primary and lower secondary school children*. Nairobi, KNAAAS, 1980.

22. Adeniji, A. *and* Issah, M.S. National Library of Nigeria; functions and achievements. *Libri*, 36, 1986. 136–145. p 143.

23. Babs Fafunwe, A. *and* Aisiku, J.U. *eds. Education in Africa: a comparative study*. London, Allen & Unwin, 1982.

24. Court, D. *and* Kinyanjui, K. African education: problems in a high growth sector. *In*: Berg, R.J. *and* Whitaker, J.S. *eds. Strategies for African development*. Berkeley, University of California Press, 1986. 361–392.

25. NEIDA. (Network of Educational Innovation for Development in Africa). *Education and productive work in Africa: a regional survey*. Dakar, Unesco Regional Office for Education in Africa, 1982.

26. Behrman, J.R. Schooling in developing countries. *Economics of Education Review*, 6, 1987. 111–127.

27. Williams, P. African education under siege. *In*: Hawes, H. *and others. Educational Priorities and Aid Responses in Sub-Saharan Africa*. London, ODA, 1986. 91–105.

28. Foster, P. The contribution of education to development. *In*: Psacharopoulos, G. *Economics of Education: Research and Studies*. London, Pergamon, 1987. 93–100. p 100.

29. NEIDA. *op. cit.*

30. Ourgay, M. Follow up materials for literacy retention and continuing education: the case of Ethiopia. *In*: Asamani, J.O. *and others eds. Libraries and Literacy. Proceedings of the 7th Meeting of the Standing Conference of Eastern, Central and Southern African Librarians, Gaborone, 4–8 August, 1986*. Gaborone, Botswana Library Association, 1987. 95–101.

31. Ourgay, M. *op. cit.* p 100.

32. Nindi, J. Some constraints for production, publication, and distribution of reading materials, especially rural newspapers, for new readers: Tanzania case study. *In*: Asamani, J.O. *and others, eds. op. cit.* 79–87.

33. Olden, A. Constraints on the development of public library service in Nigeria. *Library Quarterly*, 55, 1985. p 418.

34. Nindi, J. *op. cit.*

35. Botswana Library Association. *Report of the Conference on Libraries and Literacy*. (Kanye, April, 1985). Gaborone, Botswana Library Association, 1985.

36. Obiagwu, M.C. Foreign exchange and library collections in Nigeria. *Information Development*, 3, 1987. 154–160.

37. Saracevic, T. Consolidation of information: a concept of needed information products and services for developing countries. *ASIS Proceedings* (48th Annual Meeting, 1985), 22, 1985. 150–154.

38. Kennington, D. Geological survey libraries. *UNESCO Bulletin for Libraries*, 22, 1967. 17–21.

39. Oladele, B. A. Toward an integrated agricultural information consolidated scheme for farmers in the Nigerian rural areas. *Quarterly Bulletin of*

the International Association of Agricultural Librarians and Documentalists, 32, 1987. 98–101.

40. Nzotta, B. C. Providing information for research: Federal Research Institute Libraries in Nigeria. *Information Development*, 1, 1985. 223–228.

41. Surveys by: Adimorah, E.N.O. Users and their information needs in Nigeria. *Nigerian Library and Information Science Review*, 1, 1983. 137–148. Aina, L.O. Information needs and information-seeking involvement of farmers in six rural communities in Nigeria. *Quarterly Bulletin of the International Association of Agricultural Librarians and Documentalists*, 30, 1985. 35–40.

42. Namponya, C.R. Agricultural development and library services. *International Library Review*, 18, 1986. 267–274. p 272.

43. Saracevic, T. Progress in documentation: perception of the needs for scientific and technical information in less developed countries. *Journal of Documentation*, 36, 1980. 214–267. p 235.

44. Rosenberg, D. Repackaging scientific and technical information for illiterate and semi-literate users: a case study of the southern Sudan. *In*: Asamani, J.O. *and others eds. op. cit.* 8–22.

45. Aina, L.O. Grey literature and agricultural research in Nigeria. *Quarterly Bulletin of the International Association of Agricultural Librarians and Documentalists*, 32, 1987. 47–50.

46. Boadi, B.Y. The information sector in the economic development of Africa: the potential role for libraries. *IFLA Journal*, 10, 1984. 139–144.

Select Bibliography

Abate, D. Libraries and information services in a changing world: the challenges African information services face at the end of the 1980s. Paper presented at IFLA General Conference, Brighton, U.K., August, 1987.

Aboyade, B.O. Communications potentials of the library for non-literates—an experiment in providing information services in a rural setting. *Libri*, 34, 1984. 243–262.

Aboyade, B.O. ed. *Education and training for library and information services in a predominantly non-literate society*. The Hague, FID, 1981.

Aboyade, B.O. *Provision of information for rural development*. Ibadan, Fountain Publications, 1987.

Adeniji, A. *and* Issah, M.S. National Library of Nigeria: functions and achievements. *Libri*, 36, 1986. 136–145.

Adimorah, E.N.O. An analysis of progress made by public libraries as social institutions in Nigeria. *Unesco Journal of Information Science, Librarianship and Archives Administration*, 5, 1983. 160–167.

Adimorah, E.N.O. Information and documentation for integrated rural development in Africa. *Quarterly Bulletin of the International Association of Agricultural Librarians and Documentalists*, 29, 1984. 21–28.

Aguolu, C.C. Staffing in Nigerian university libraries. *Library Review*, 31, 1982. 18–29.

Aina, L.O. Agricultural information provision in Nigeria. *Information Development*, 2, 1986. 242–244.

Aina, L.O. Grey literature and agricultural research in Nigeria. *Quarterly Bulletin of the International Association of Agricultural Librarians and Documentalists*, 32, 1987. 47–50.

Aina, L.O. Information needs and information seeking involvement of farmers in six rural communities in Nigeria. *Quarterly Bulletin of the International Association of Agricultural Librarians and Documentalists*, 30, 1985. 35–40.

Aithnard, K.M. Is the library a source of information in the developing countries? Paper presented at IFLA General Conference, Brighton, U.K., August, 1987.

Aiyepeku, W.O. Information transfer: implications of development research in administration in Nigeria. *Public Administration and Development*, 3, 1983. 161–172.

Aiyepeku, W.O. Information utilization by policy makers in Nigeria. *Journal of Information Science*, 4, 1982. 203–211.

Aiyepeku, W.O. *International socio-economic information system: an evaluation of DEVSIS-type programs.* Ottawa, International Development Research Centre, 1983.

Ajia, S.A. *British aid to Nigerian libraries: an analytical study of the work of three major British organisations involved in the development of library services in the country.* Unpublished Ph.D. Thesis, Loughborough University of Technology, 1983.

Akam, A.A. Information system for planning in Ghana. *Planning and Administration*, 9, 1982. 113–127.

Alegbeleye, G.O. The non-use of Nigerian public libraries by the silent majority: a historical survey and discursus. *Libri*, 36, 1986. 187–201.

Altbach, P.G., Arboleda, A.A. *and* Gopinathan, S. *eds. Publishing in the Third World: knowledge and development.* London, Mansell, 1985.

Amaratunga, C. *and* Shute, J. Extension and adult learning in a Ghanaian community. *Canadian Journal of African Studies*, 16, 1982. 549–566.

Ambrose, D.P. Collection and bibliographical control of grey literature of Lesotho. *African Research and Documentation*, 36, 1984. 11–24.

Amin, S. *Imperialism and unequal development.* New York, Monthly Review Press, 1977.

Amon, B. *and* Lajeunesse, M. Les bibliothèques universitaires en Afrique de l'Ouest francophone: problèmes et perspectives. *Libri*, 37, 1987. 109–125.

Anheier, H.K. *and* Seibel, H.D. *Small scale industries and economic development in Ghana: business behavior and strategies in informal sector economies.* Saarbrucken, Breitenbach, 1987. (Cologne Development Studies, 3).

Asamani, J.O. *and others eds. Libraries and literacy. Proceedings of the 7th Standing Conference of the Eastern Central and Southern African Librarians (SCECSAL) Gaborone, 4–8 August, 1986.* Gaborone, Botswana Library Association, 1987.

Balabkins, N.W. Collecting information in a developing country. *Harvard Library Bulletin*, 32, 1984. 54–72.

Behrman, J.R. Schooling in developing countries. *Economics of Education Review*, 6, 1987. 111–127.

Benge, R.C. *Cultural crisis and libraries in the Third World.* London, Bingley, 1979.

Bhola, H.S. *and* Bhola, J.K. *Planning and organisation of literacy campaigns. Programs and projects.* Bonn, DSE, 1984.

Boadi, B. The information sector in the economic development of Africa: the potential role for libraries. *IFLA Journal*, 10, 1984. 137–144.

Boafo, S.T.K. Utilising development communication strategies in African societies: a critical perspective. *Gazette. International Journal for Mass Communication Studies*, 35, 1985. 83–92.

Bock, G. *and* Huttemann, L. *eds. Curriculum adjustments in information studies training programmes in Africa.* Bonn, DSE, 1987.

Botswana Library Association. *Report of the Conference on Libraries and Literacy, Kanye, April 1985.* Gaborone, Botswana Library Association, 1985.

Brewster, B. *American overseas library technical assistance, 1940-1970*. Metuchen, N.J., Scarecrow Press, 1976.

Browne, R.S. *The Lagos Plan of Action versus the Berg Report*. Lawrenceville, Va., Brunswick Publishing Co., 1984.

Bude, U. *Primary schools, local community, and development in Africa*. Baden-Baden, Nomus Verlagsgesellschaft, 1985.

Byram, M.L. Odi Weavers: material culture, workers organization, and nonformal education in Botswana. *In*: Kidd, R. *and* Colletta, N. *eds. Tradition for development: indigenous structures and folk media in non-formal education*. Berlin, DSE, 1980. 207-244.

Carron, G. *and* Bordia, A. *eds. Issues in planning and implementing national literacy programmes*. Paris, Unesco, 1985.

Chakava, H. Reading in Africa—some obstacles. *IFLA Journal*, 10, 1984. 348-356.

Coombs, D. *Spreading the word: the library work of the British Council*. London, Mansell, 1988.

Court, D. *and* Kinyanjui, K. African education: problems in a high growth sector. *In*: Berg, R.J. *and* Whitaker, J.S. *eds. Strategies for African development*. Berkeley, University of California Press, 1986.

Craver, K.W. Survey of library services to children and young adults in selected countries in Africa and Asia. *Top of the News*, 41, 1985. 33-43.

Crowder, M. The book crisis: Africa's other famine. *African Research and Documentation*, 41, 1986. 1-6.

Cutter, C.H. Political communication in a preliterate society: the example of rural Mali. *Rural Africana*, 27, 1975. 9-23.

Demol, E., Nihan, G. *and* Jondoh, C. Lome's industrial sector. *In*: Fransman, M. *ed. Industry and accumulation in Africa*. London, Heinemann, 1982. 354-371.

Domatob, J.K. Communication for self-reliance in Black Africa. *Gazette. International Journal for Mass Communication Studies*, 40, 1987. 167-182.

Doob, L.W. *Communication in Africa*. New Haven, Yale University Press, 1961.

Durrani, S. Rural information in Kenya. *Information Development*, 1, 1985. 149-157.

Easterbrook, D.L. INFOTRAC and Africa. *African Research and Documentation*, 44, 1987. 12-15.

Eicher, C.K. *International technology transfer and the African farmer: theory and practice*. Harare, Department of Land Management, University of Zimbabwe, 1984. (Working Paper 3/84).

Eicher, C.K. *and* Baker, D.C. *Research on agricultural development in sub-Saharan Africa: a critical survey*. East Lansing, Department of Agricultural Economics, Michigan State University, 1982. (MSU International Development Paper 1).

Escarpit, R. *Trends in worldwide book development, 1970-1978*. Paris, Unesco, 1982.

Fiofori, D. Traditional media and modern messages: a Nigerian study. *Rural Africana*, 27, 1975. 43-52.

Foster, P. The contribution of education to development. *In*: Psacharopoulos,

G. *ed. Economics of education: research and studies.* London, Pergamon, 1987. 93–100.

Fransman, M. *Technology and economic development.* Brighton, Wheatsheaf, 1986.

Gehrke, U. Information for development. Some problems of national co-ordination, regional co-ordination and international assistance. *INSPEL*, 9, 1985. 166–198.

Gifford, C.A. Closing the gap: the New World Information Order. *Africa Report*, 32, 1987. 81–84.

Goody, J. *ed. Literacy in traditional society.* Cambridge, Cambridge University Press, 1968.

Green, R.H. *and* Allison, C. The World Bank's agenda for accelerated development: dialectics, doubts, and dialogues. *In*: Ravenhill, J. *ed. Africa in economic crisis.* London, Macmillan, 1986. 50–84.

Gunton, D. *Books, libraries and aid, in particular British aid in Nigeria during the development decade 1960–1969.* Unpublished M.A. Thesis, University of Sheffield, 1974.

Haule, J.J. Old paradigm and new order in the African context: toward an appropriate model of communication and national development. *Gazette. International Journal for Mass Communication Studies*, 33, 1984. 3–15.

Hayward, F.M. A reassessment of the conventional wisdom about the informed public. National political information in Ghana. *American Political Science Review*, 70, 1976. 433–451.

Hill, P. *Development economics on trial: the anthropological case for a prosecution.* Cambridge, Cambridge University Press, 1986.

Huttemann, L. *ed. Establishment and management of a national information service in Botswana.* Bonn/Gaborone, DSE/ Botswana National Library Service, 1987.

Irele, A. An African perspective of publishing for African Studies. *In*: Sternberg, I. *and* Larby, P.M. *eds. African Studies. Papers presented at a colloquium at the British Library, 7–9 January, 1985.* London, British Library, 1986. 77–89.

Kamba, A.S. Archives and national development in the Third World. *Information Development*, 3, 1987. 108–113.

Kaungamno, E.E. *and* Ilomo, J.S. *Books build nations.* 2 vols. Dar es Salaam, TransAfrica, 1979.

Kenya National Academy for Advancement of Arts and Science. *A survey of reading habits and preferences among Nairobi primary and lower secondary school children.* Nairobi, KNAAAS, 1980.

Kerr, D. Didactic theatre in Africa. *Harvard Educational Review*, 31, 1981. 145–155.

Kibirigi, H. Libraries and illiteracy in developing countries: a critical assessment. *Libri* 27, 1977. 54–67.

Kotei, S.I.A. *The book today in Africa.* Paris, Unesco, 1981.

Kotei, S.I.A. Some cultural and social factors of book reading and publishing in Africa. *In*: Oluwasanmi, E., McLean, E. *and* Zell, H. *eds. Publishing in Africa in the seventies.* Ife, University of Ife Press, 1975. 174–208.

Kotei, S.I.A. Some variables of comparison between developed and developing library systems. *International Library Review*, 9, 1977. 249–267.

Lele, U. *Design of rural development: lessons from Africa.* Baltimore, Johns Hopkins University Press, 1975.

Lewycky, D. *Tapestry—report from Odi Weavers.* Gaborone, National Institute of Research, 1977.

Livingstone, I. Alternative approaches to small industry promotion. *In*: Fransman, M. *Industry and accumulation in Africa.* London, Heinemann, 1982. 354–371.

Lundu, M.C. Library education and training: at home or abroad? *International Library Review*, 14, 1982. 363–378.

Lungu, C.M. Resource sharing and self-reliance in Southern Africa. *Information Development*, 3, 1987. 82–86.

Maack, M.N. The colonial legacy in West African libraries: a comparative study. *In*: Simonton, W. *ed. Advances in Librarianship. Vol. 12.* New York, Academic Press, 1982. 174–245.

Maack, M.N. The role of external aid in West African library development. *Library Quarterly*, 56, 1986. 1–16.

McAnany, E.G. New approaches to development: does information really work? *Journal of Communication*, 28, 1978. 84–90.

McCarthy, C. Colonial cataloguing. *New Library World*, 76, 1975. 55.

Mazikana, P.C. Archives and oral history: overcoming a lack of resources. *Information Development*, 3, 1987. 13–16.

Mazrui, A.A. The computer culture and nuclear power: political implications for Africa. *In*: Shaw, T.M. *ed. Alternative futures for Africa.* Boulder, Colorado, Westview Press, 1982. 237–258.

Mazrui, A.A. *and* Tidy, M. *Nationalism and new states in Africa.* Nairobi, Heinemann, 1984.

Mchombu, K.J. On the librarianship of poverty. *Libri*, 32, 1982. 241–250.

Meillassoux, C. *ed. Maidens, meal and money: capitalism and the domestic community.* Cambridge, Cambridge University Press, 1981.

Membury, D. The Ranfurly Library Service and the Textbooks for Africa Project. *African Research and Documentation*, 46, 1988. 40–46.

Msiska, A.W.C. Early attempts at creating African literature: its distribution, local authorship and library service in Northern Rhodesia (Zambia) and Nyasaland (Malawi). *Libri*, 36, 1986. 240–246.

Munslow, B. and Pycroft, C. The Southern African Computerised Data/Text (SACDT) system. *African Research and Documentation*, 45, 1988. 9–14.

Namponya, C.R. Agricultural development and library services. *International Library Review*, 18, 1986. 267–274.

Ndiaye, R. Oral culture and libraries. *IFLA Journal*, 14, 1988. 40–46.

Nduntuei, O.I. Some problems of bibliographic control in Nigeria. *Libri*, 36, 1986. 320–335.

NEIDA (Network of Educational Innovation for Development in Africa). *Education and productive work in Africa: a regional survey.* Dakar, Unesco Regional Office for Education In Africa, 1982.

Neill, J.R. Library manpower planning in Southern, Central, and Eastern Africa. *In*: Huttemann, L. *ed. Manpower training needs. Proceedings and papers of the Information Experts Meeting, Harare, Zimbabwe, April, 1985.* Bonn, DSE, 1985. 19–28.

Nwafor, B.U. Problems of the book trade infrastructure in developing countries in relation to university library objectives. *IFLA Journal*, 10, 1984. 357–369.

Nwuneli, O.E. *and* Udoh, E. International news coverage in Nigerian newspapers. *Gazette. International Journal for Mass Communication Studies*, 29, 1982. 31–40.

Obasi, J.U. Bibliographical control of Nigerian publications: social science primary materials. *Journal of Documentation*, 38, 1982. 107–124.

Obi, D. Education for rural library service in Africa. *Rural Africana* (New Series) 1, 1978. 67–68.

Obiagwu, M.C. Foreign exchange and library collections in Nigeria. *Information Development*, 3, 1987. 154–160.

Obiechina, E. *An African popular literature: a study of Onitsha market pamphlets*. Cambridge, Cambridge University Press, 1973.

Odumosu, M.O. Mass media and immunization of pregnant women in a Nigerian community. *Canadian Journal of Public Health*, 73, 1982. 105–108.

Oladele, B.A. Toward an integrated agricultural consolidated scheme for farmers in the Nigerian rural areas. *Quarterly Bulletin of the International Association of Agricultural Librarians and Documentalists*, 32, 1987. 98–101.

Olden, A. *The beneficiaries of library and information policy in British and ex-British Africa*. Unpublished Ph.D. Thesis, University of Illinois, at Urbana-Champaign, 1987.

Olden, A. Constraints on the development of public library service in Nigeria. *Library Quarterly*, 55, 1985. 398–423.

Olden, A. Sub-Saharan Africa and the paperless society. *Journal of the American Society for Information Science*, 38, 1987. 298–304.

Oluwasanmi, E., McLean, E., *and* Zell, H. *eds. Publishing in Africa in the seventies*. Ife, University of Ife Press, 1975.

Omotoso, K. Writing rights and wrongs for our children. *In*: Dillsworth, G. *ed. Seminar on creative writing and publishing for children in Africa today*. Freetown, Sierra Leone Library Board, 1983. 5–12.

Organization of African Unity. *Lagos Plan of Action for the Economic Development of Africa, 1980–2000*. Geneva, International Institute for Labour Studies, 1981.

Osa, O. *Nigerian youth literature*. Benin City, Paramount Publishers, 1987.

Parker, J.S. *Unesco and library development planning*. London, Library Association, 1985.

Porat, M.U. Global implications of the information society. *Journal of Communication*, 28, 1978. 70–80.

Pratt, C. Communicating population issues in sub-Saharan Africa: a development policy for Nigeria. *Gazette. International Journal for Mass Communication Studies*, 37, 1986. 169–189.

Rahard, M. *and* Bourdin, J.F. FRANCIS can inform you on Africa. *African Research and Documentation*, 42, 1985. 8–19.

Rahnema, M. The sound library, a simple but revolutionary tool for development. *Unesco Journal of Information Science, Librarianship and Archives Administration*, 4, 1982. 151–158.

Raseroka, H.K. Relevant library services in developing countries. *IFLA Journal*, 12, 1986. 288–291.

Rathgeber, E.M. Africana acquisitions problems: the view from both sides. *Library Acquisitions Practice and Theory*, 6, 1982. 137–148.

Renaud, J.C. A revised agenda for the New World Information Order: the transborder data flow issue. *Gazette. International Journal for Mass Communication Studies*, 34, 1984. 117–135.

Roberts, K.H. ed. *Regional postgraduate program in information science in Anglophone Africa: identification of an appropriate location. Report of a joint Unesco/IDRC mission*. Ottawa, IDRC, 1986.

Roling, N. Knowledge brokerage for increasing the relevance of agricultural research to African smallholders. *Rural Africana*, 27, 1975. 113–119.

Samaha, E.K. Document delivery: the AGRIS cooperative solution. *Information Development*, 3, 1987. 103–107.

Saracevic, T. Progress in documentation: perception of the needs for scientific and technical information in less developed countries. *Journal of Documentation*, 36, 1980. 214–267.

Scheub, H. A review of African oral traditions and literature. *African Studies Review*, 28, 1985. 1–72.

Shio, M. *and* Musana, A. *Evaluation of user seminars conducted in Tanzania, Zambia, Malawi, Lesotho, Swaziland, Botswana*. Bonn, DSE, 1981.

Sly, M. Improving accessibility to development literature. *Library Acquisitions Practice and Theory*, 6, 1982. 117–122.

Stolper, W.F. *Planning without facts: lessons in resource allocation from Nigeria's development*. Cambridge, Mass., Harvard University Press, 1966.

Sturges, P. International transfer of information and national self-sufficiency: the case of Botswana. *In: Proceedings of the Annual Meeting of the American Society for Information Science. Chicago, Sept. 1986, vol. 23*. Knowledge Industry Publications, 1986. 320–325.

Sturges, P. What librarians feel about their careers: a survey of diploma and certificate holders. *Botswana Library Association Journal*, 7, 1985. 9–21.

Thairu, R.W. Cataloguing policies and problems in Kenyan libraries. *African Research and Documentation*, 40, 1986. 8–15.

Thurston, A. The Zanzibar Archives project. *Information Development*, 2, 1986. 223–226.

Tocatlian, J. *and* Abid, A. The development of library and information services in developing countries: Unesco/ PGI's role and activities. *IFLA Journal*, 12, 1986. 280–285.

Ugboajah, F.O. ed. *Mass communication, culture and society in West Africa*. London, Hans Zell, 1985.

Ume-Nwagbo, E.N. Foreign news flows in Africa: a content analytical study on a regional basis. *Gazette. International Journal for Mass Communication Studies*, 29, 1982. 41–56.

Unesco. *Development of public libraries in Africa: the Ibadan Seminar*. Paris, Unesco, 1954. (Public Library Manuals no. 6).

Unesco. *Expert meeting on national planning of documentation library services in Africa. Kampala, Uganda, 7–15 Dec., 1970*. Paris, Unesco, 1971.

Unesco. *An international survey of book production during the last decade*. Paris, Unesco, 1982.

Unesco. *Meeting of experts on planning documentation and library networks in Africa*

(NATIS). Brazzaville, People's Republic of Congo, 5–10 July, 1976. Paris, Unesco, 1975.

Vansina, J. *Oral tradition as history*. Madison, University of Wisconsin Press, 1985.

Wauthier, C. PANA the voice of Africa. *Africa Report*, 32, 1987. 65–67.

Williams, P. African education under siege. *In*: Hawes, H. *and others, eds. Education priorities and aid responses in sub-Saharan Africa*. London, Office of Overseas Development, 1986. 91–105.

Wolke-Renk, I.D. Acquisition of African literature. *IFLA Journal*, 10, 1984. 377–384.

World Bank. *Accelerated development in sub-Saharan Africa: an agenda for action*. Washington, D.C., World Bank, 1981.

Zell, H.M. African scholarly publishing in the eighties. *Scholarly Publishing*, 18, 1987. 97–102.

Zell, H.M. The other famine. *Libri*, 37, 1987. 294–306.

Index

169